KUBERNETES
INTERVIEW QUESTIONS
AND
ANSWERS

50 Essential Questions to Ace Your Interview

MAXWELL RIVERS

CONTENTS

1 INTRODUCTION

As Kubernetes continues to gain momentum in the world of DevOps and cloud-native computing, it has become a critical skill for technology professionals and a key focus of interviews for roles in system administration, DevOps, and cloud architecture.

If you're reading this book, chances are you're either preparing for a Kubernetes-related job interview or aiming to strengthen your understanding of Kubernetes. Regardless of your motivation, you've come to the right place. This book, "Top 50 Kubernetes Interview Questions and Answers," is designed to be your comprehensive guide to mastering Kubernetes interview concepts and techniques.

Why Kubernetes Matters

Before we delve into the depths of Kubernetes interview questions, it's crucial to grasp why Kubernetes has become a cornerstone technology in the world of containers and cloud-native computing.

Kubernetes provides a robust framework for automating the deployment, scaling, and management of containerized applications. Whether you're dealing with a single-container application or a complex microservices architecture, Kubernetes simplifies the orchestration of containers, ensuring high availability, scalability, and resilience. Its declarative configuration model, combined with a rich set of abstractions, allows you to define your application's desired state and let Kubernetes handle the complexities of maintaining that state.

The benefits of Kubernetes extend beyond technical advantages. Organizations that embrace Kubernetes can accelerate their development and release cycles, enhance resource utilization, reduce operational overhead, and future-proof their applications by adhering to cloud-native best practices.

Navigating This Book

This book is structured to provide you with a comprehensive understanding of Kubernetes interview topics. Each chapter focuses on specific aspects of Kubernetes, from its fundamental components and architecture to advanced topics like security, scaling, and troubleshooting. Within each chapter, we present a set of essential interview questions followed by detailed answers and explanations. These questions are carefully selected to cover a broad range of Kubernetes concepts and real-world scenarios.

Whether you're a beginner looking to grasp the fundamentals of Kubernetes or an experienced practitioner seeking to fine-tune your knowledge for interviews, you'll find valuable insights and practical guidance within these pages. Our aim is to equip you with the knowledge and confidence needed to excel in Kubernetes-related interviews and succeed in your career.

The journey to Kubernetes mastery begins here. Each question you encounter in this book is an opportunity to expand your knowledge and gain a deeper understanding of Kubernetes. Remember that Kubernetes is a dynamic field, with new features and best practices continually emerging. By the time you reach the final page, you'll be well-prepared to tackle Kubernetes-related interviews and contribute effectively to projects involving container orchestration.

What is Kubernetes, and why is it important?

Kubernetes is an open-source container orchestration platform that automates the deployment, scaling, management, and orchestration of containerized applications. Originally developed by Google and later handed over to the Cloud Native Computing Foundation (CNCF), Kubernetes has become the de facto standard for container orchestration in the world of cloud-native computing. It provides a powerful framework for managing containerized workloads and services, offering a range of benefits for both developers and operations teams.

Here's why Kubernetes is important:

1. **Container Orchestration:** Kubernetes simplifies the management of containerized applications. Containers package an application and its dependencies into a single unit, making it easy to deploy consistently across different environments. Kubernetes extends this by automating tasks like scaling, load balancing, and rolling updates, saving significant time and effort.
2. **Scalability:** Kubernetes allows you to effortlessly scale your applications up or down based on demand. It can automatically distribute containerized workloads across available resources, ensuring optimal resource utilization and improved application performance.
3. **High Availability:** Kubernetes provides built-in mechanisms for ensuring the high availability of applications. It can automatically detect and recover from node failures, move workloads to healthy nodes, and maintain the desired state of applications, minimizing downtime.
4. **Declarative Configuration:** With Kubernetes, you define the desired state of your applications and infrastructure using declarative configuration files (YAML). Kubernetes continuously monitors the actual state and makes adjustments to match the desired state, simplifying configuration management and reducing human error.
5. **Ecosystem Integration:** Kubernetes has a rich ecosystem of tools and services that can be seamlessly integrated to enhance its capabilities. This includes monitoring and logging solutions,

continuous integration and continuous deployment (CI/CD) pipelines, and various storage options, among others.

6. **Portability:** Kubernetes offers a consistent platform for deploying and managing applications across different cloud providers and on-premises data centers. This portability helps organizations avoid vendor lock-in and adapt to changing infrastructure needs.

7. **Community Support:** Kubernetes boasts a large and active open-source community, which means constant development, improvement, and support. This collaborative ecosystem ensures that Kubernetes remains up-to-date with the latest industry best practices and emerging technologies.

8. **Cloud-Native Computing:** Kubernetes aligns with cloud-native principles, making it an ideal choice for building and running applications designed for the cloud. It promotes microservices architecture, which allows for greater agility, scalability, and resilience in modern software development.

9. **Cost Efficiency:** By optimizing resource usage and automating many operational tasks, Kubernetes can help reduce infrastructure costs. It allows organizations to maximize the efficiency of their cloud resources or on-premises hardware.

10. **Innovation and Future-Proofing:** Kubernetes is at the forefront of technology innovation, enabling organizations to stay competitive by embracing the latest trends in containerization, serverless computing, and cloud-native technologies. It positions companies for future growth and adaptability in a rapidly evolving tech landscape.

How does Kubernetes help in container orchestration?

Kubernetes plays a pivotal role in container orchestration by providing a robust framework for automating the deployment, scaling, management, and coordination of containerized applications. Here's how Kubernetes helps in container orchestration:

1. **Automated Deployment:** Kubernetes simplifies the deployment process by defining containers, their configurations, and interdependencies in declarative configuration files. Once defined, Kubernetes takes care of launching and distributing containers across the cluster, ensuring that the desired number of instances is running.

2. **Scalability:** Kubernetes enables automatic scaling of containerized applications based on resource utilization or predefined metrics. It can scale applications both horizontally (adding more container instances) and vertically (resizing individual containers), allowing applications to handle varying workloads efficiently.

3. **Load Balancing:** Kubernetes offers built-in load balancing for services, distributing incoming network traffic across multiple containers or Pods. This ensures even distribution of requests and prevents overloading of any single instance, enhancing application availability and performance.

4. **Service Discovery:** Kubernetes provides a DNS-based service discovery mechanism, allowing containers to locate and communicate with other services within the cluster using service names rather than hard-coded IP addresses. This dynamic service discovery simplifies application configuration.

5. **Health Checking:** Kubernetes regularly checks the health of containers and Pods. Unhealthy containers are automatically terminated and replaced with healthy ones, ensuring that applications are running reliably.

6. **Rolling Updates and Rollbacks:** Kubernetes supports rolling updates, enabling seamless updates of applications without downtime. It gradually replaces old container instances with new ones, monitoring their health throughout the process. In case of issues, Kubernetes allows for quick rollbacks to a previous stable version.

7. **Resource Management:** Kubernetes efficiently manages cluster resources, including CPU and memory, by allocating resources to containers based on resource requests and limits. This prevents one container from monopolizing resources and ensures fair resource sharing.

8. **Self-Healing:** Kubernetes automatically detects and recovers from container and node failures. If a container or node becomes

unavailable, Kubernetes reschedules containers to healthy nodes, maintaining application availability.

9. **Declarative Configuration:** Kubernetes uses declarative configuration files (YAML or JSON) to specify the desired state of applications and infrastructure. It continuously reconciles the actual state with the desired state, making necessary adjustments to ensure consistency.

10. **Storage Orchestration:** Kubernetes manages storage for containers, supporting various storage solutions. It can provision and attach storage volumes to containers, ensuring that data persists even if containers are rescheduled or replaced.

11. **Networking:** Kubernetes configures and manages networking for containers, allowing them to communicate within and outside the cluster. It supports various network models, including overlay networks and container-to-container networking.

12. **Security:** Kubernetes provides features like Role-Based Access Control (RBAC), pod security policies, and network policies to enhance the security of containerized applications. It isolates workloads, controls access, and enforces security policies.

13. **Extensibility:** Kubernetes is highly extensible and allows you to integrate additional components and services to enhance its functionality. The Kubernetes ecosystem includes a wide range of add-ons and plugins for various purposes.

2 KUBERNETES BASICS

What are containers, and how do they relate to Kubernetes?

Containers are lightweight, standalone, and executable packages that contain everything needed to run a piece of software, including the code, runtime, libraries, and system tools. Containers offer a consistent and isolated environment for applications, making it possible to develop, package, and deploy software across different computing environments with confidence.

Now, let's explore how containers relate to Kubernetes:

1. **Containerization Technology:** Containers are the building blocks of containerization technology, and they serve as the foundation for Kubernetes. Containers provide a standardized format for packaging applications and their dependencies, ensuring that they run consistently across various environments.
2. **Application Packaging:** Kubernetes leverages containers as the primary packaging format for applications. In Kubernetes, containers are encapsulated within units called "Pods," which are the smallest deployable units. A Pod can contain one or more containers that work together as part of the same application or service.

3. **Deployment Units:** Kubernetes uses containers as the primary deployment unit. You define how many instances of a containerized application you want to run using Kubernetes resources, such as Deployments or StatefulSets. Kubernetes then manages the creation, scaling, and termination of these containers to meet your desired state.

4. **Scaling:** Containers are instrumental in enabling Kubernetes to scale applications efficiently. Kubernetes can easily replicate container instances to handle increased workloads. This scalability is achieved by creating additional container instances (Pods) based on the container image you've defined.

5. **Resource Isolation:** Containers provide resource isolation for applications, ensuring that each container runs independently of others on the same host. Kubernetes extends this isolation by scheduling containers on different nodes within a cluster, enhancing security and reliability.

6. **Networking:** Containers within the same Pod share the same network namespace, allowing them to communicate with each other over localhost. Kubernetes manages networking for Pods, enabling communication between containers in different Pods and external clients. This network abstraction simplifies service discovery and load balancing.

7. **Portability:** Containers, including their applications and dependencies, are encapsulated in a single package. This portability allows you to develop and test applications locally in a containerized environment and then deploy them consistently across various Kubernetes clusters, cloud providers, or on-premises data centers.

8. **Lifecycle Management:** Kubernetes takes care of the lifecycle management of containerized applications. It automates tasks such as deployment, scaling, rolling updates, and self-healing, ensuring that your applications run reliably and efficiently.

9. **Resource Management:** Kubernetes manages the allocation of CPU and memory resources to containers, allowing you to specify resource requests and limits for each container. This resource control prevents one container from consuming all available resources, ensuring fair resource sharing.

What are Pods in Kubernetes?

In Kubernetes, a **Pod** is the smallest deployable unit and the fundamental building block of containerized applications. A Pod can contain one or more containers that are scheduled together on the same host and share the same network namespace. While containers within the same Pod share network and storage resources, each container has its own file system, process space, and system libraries, providing a level of isolation.

Here are key points to understand about Pods in Kubernetes:

1. **Atomic Unit:** Pods are the atomic units of deployment in Kubernetes. When you want to run one or more containers together as a single unit, you define them within the same Pod. Containers within a Pod are scheduled together on the same node and share the same lifecycle.
2. **Shared Network Namespace:** Containers within a Pod share the same network namespace, which means they can communicate with each other over localhost (127.0.0.1). This shared network namespace simplifies inter-container communication within the same Pod.
3. **Shared Storage Volume:** Pods can define shared storage volumes that are mounted into all containers within the Pod. This allows containers to share data or configuration files.
4. **Use Cases:** Pods are commonly used to encapsulate tightly coupled application components that need to run together on the same host. For example, a web application may have a Pod with two containers: one running the web server and another running a sidecar container for logging.
5. **Single IP Address:** Each Pod is assigned a unique IP address within the cluster's network. This IP address is reachable from other Pods within the same cluster, but it may not be reachable from outside the cluster without additional configuration.
6. **Scaling Pods:** To scale an application horizontally, you can create multiple identical Pods. Kubernetes manages the distribution of these Pods across different nodes in the cluster to ensure high availability and load balancing.

7. **Pod Lifecycle:** Pods have a lifecycle that includes phases like "Pending," "Running," "Succeeded," "Failed," or "Unknown." Kubernetes continuously monitors the state of Pods and takes actions to maintain the desired state.

8. **Immutable:** Once a Pod is created, it is considered immutable. If you need to update the containers within a Pod, you typically create a new Pod with the updated container images and configuration, and then scale down or delete the old Pod.

9. **Controllers:** In practice, Pods are often managed and created by higher-level controllers like Deployments, StatefulSets, and DaemonSets. These controllers manage the desired number of Pods, rolling updates, and other aspects of application lifecycle management.

How does Kubernetes handle container scaling?

Kubernetes provides powerful mechanisms for scaling containers, allowing you to efficiently manage the number of container instances based on workload demands. Kubernetes offers both manual and automated scaling options to ensure that your applications are appropriately sized and can adapt to changing conditions. Here's how Kubernetes handles container scaling:

1. **Horizontal Pod Autoscaling (HPA):** Kubernetes offers Horizontal Pod Autoscaling (HPA) as an automated way to scale containers based on CPU utilization or custom metrics. You define target metrics and thresholds, and Kubernetes automatically adjusts the number of Pods to meet the specified targets. For example, if CPU utilization exceeds a certain threshold, Kubernetes will create additional Pods to handle the increased load.

2. **Cluster Autoscaler:** To handle situations where you need more nodes in your cluster due to resource constraints, Kubernetes provides the Cluster Autoscaler. This component can automatically adjust the size of the cluster by adding or removing

nodes based on resource demands. This ensures that your cluster can accommodate the scaled Pods.

3. **Vertical Pod Autoscaling (VPA):** While HPA scales the number of Pods horizontally, Vertical Pod Autoscaling (VPA) focuses on adjusting the CPU and memory resource requests for individual Pods. VPA evaluates the resource utilization of Pods and recommends resource requests and limits that better match their actual usage, helping to optimize resource allocation.

4. **Manual Scaling:** Kubernetes allows manual scaling through the use of commands or configuration updates. You can manually adjust the desired number of replicas for a Deployment, StatefulSet, or ReplicaSet to increase or decrease the number of running Pods. While manual, this approach offers fine-grained control over scaling.

5. **Desired State Management:** Kubernetes continually compares the desired state (specified in the resource definition, e.g., a Deployment) with the current state of the cluster. If there's a discrepancy (e.g., fewer Pods than desired), Kubernetes automatically takes corrective actions by creating new Pods or terminating excess ones to match the desired state.

6. **Load Balancing:** Kubernetes automatically distributes incoming traffic across the available Pods for a service. As you scale up or down, the load balancer ensures that requests are evenly distributed to the newly created or removed Pods, maintaining application availability.

7. **Rolling Updates:** When you perform rolling updates to your application, Kubernetes gradually replaces old Pods with new ones. This allows you to update your application without causing downtime. The rollout strategy ensures that a specified number of new Pods are created before old Pods are terminated.

8. **Pod Disruption Budgets:** To ensure that your application remains stable during scaling or maintenance operations, you can define Pod Disruption Budgets. These policies specify the maximum allowed disruption to Pods within a certain category, helping to prevent excessive scaling or disruptions that could impact availability.

9. **Custom Metrics:** In addition to CPU and memory metrics, Kubernetes allows you to define custom metrics for autoscaling. This feature enables more advanced autoscaling based on

application-specific metrics such as request latency, queue depth, or any other metric you deem relevant.

10. **Integration with External Scaling Solutions:** Kubernetes can integrate with external scaling solutions or systems, such as the Horizontal Pod Autoscaler (HPA) working in tandem with custom metrics or external services. This flexibility allows you to tailor scaling decisions to your specific use cases.

What are Services in Kubernetes, and why are they essential?

In Kubernetes, **Services** are essential constructs that provide a stable and reliable network abstraction for accessing groups of Pods. They play a critical role in ensuring the availability, discoverability, and load balancing of containerized applications within a cluster. Here's a closer look at Services in Kubernetes and why they are vital:

Services in Kubernetes:

1. **Network Abstraction:** Services provide a consistent and abstract way to expose Pods to the network. Instead of directly connecting to individual Pods, clients can access a Service, which acts as a network endpoint. This abstraction shields clients from the underlying complexity of Pod IP addresses and dynamic Pod scheduling.
2. **Stable Virtual IPs:** Each Service is associated with a stable virtual IP address (Cluster IP), which remains constant even if Pods are scaled, replaced, or rescheduled. This virtual IP is used by clients to access the Service, ensuring that the Service remains reachable regardless of Pod changes.
3. **Load Balancing:** Services automatically distribute incoming network traffic across the Pods backing the Service. This load balancing enhances application availability and performance by evenly distributing requests. Load balancing is particularly valuable when scaling Pods to handle varying workloads.
4. **Service Discovery:** Kubernetes provides DNS-based service discovery. Each Service is registered in the cluster's DNS system

using its service name. This enables other Pods and services to discover and communicate with the Service using its DNS name, simplifying service discovery within the cluster.

5. **Multiple Service Types:** Kubernetes offers various Service types to cater to different use cases:

o **ClusterIP:** Provides internal access within the cluster. It is not accessible from outside the cluster.

o **NodePort:** Exposes the Service on a specific port on all nodes in the cluster. It is suitable for applications that require external access but do not need advanced routing or domain names.

o **LoadBalancer:** Integrates with cloud provider load balancers to expose the Service externally. It provides a stable external IP address for clients.

o **ExternalName:** Maps the Service to an external DNS name. This type is used to provide access to external resources with a DNS name.

Why Services are Essential:

1. **Service Abstraction:** Services abstract the complexity of managing individual Pods and their dynamic IP addresses. This abstraction simplifies application development, as developers and clients can rely on the stable virtual IP provided by the Service.

2. **High Availability:** Services ensure that applications remain available and resilient. Even if individual Pods fail, the Service continues to route traffic to healthy Pods, minimizing downtime and disruptions.

3. **Scaling:** When you scale your application by adding more Pods, Services automatically balance the incoming traffic across the expanded set of Pods. This dynamic load balancing is crucial for efficiently distributing workloads.

4. **Service Discovery:** With DNS-based service discovery, Pods and services can locate and communicate with each other using human-readable DNS names, promoting a loosely coupled architecture. This simplifies configuration and enables dynamic service discovery as Pods come and go.

5. **Security:** Services can be configured to allow or deny traffic from specific sources, enhancing network security within the

cluster. They provide an additional layer of security by controlling access to Pods.

6. **External Access:** Services like NodePort and LoadBalancer allow applications to be exposed externally, making them accessible to users or systems outside the Kubernetes cluster. This is vital for public-facing applications.

What is a Namespace in Kubernetes, and why would you use it?

In Kubernetes, a **Namespace** is a logical and virtual cluster within a physical Kubernetes cluster. Namespaces allow you to partition a Kubernetes cluster into multiple virtual clusters, each with its own isolated resources and objects. Here's a closer look at what Namespaces are and why you would use them:

What is a Namespace in Kubernetes:

1. **Logical Partitioning:** A Namespace serves as a logical partition within a Kubernetes cluster. It acts as a container for various Kubernetes resources, such as Pods, Services, ConfigMaps, Secrets, and more. These resources are then scoped to that specific Namespace.

2. **Resource Isolation:** Resources created in one Namespace are isolated from those in other Namespaces. This means that you can have resources with the same names in different Namespaces without conflicts. For example, you can have a "web" Service in one Namespace and another "web" Service in a different Namespace.

3. **Object Namespacing:** Kubernetes objects like Pods, Services, and ConfigMaps are bound to a Namespace when created. This means that objects within a Namespace have unique names within that Namespace but can have the same names in different Namespaces.

4. **Default Namespace:** A Kubernetes cluster typically has a "default" Namespace that is used when resources are created

without specifying a Namespace. This allows you to organize resources without explicitly assigning them to a Namespace.

Why Would You Use Namespaces:

1. **Multi-Tenancy:** Namespaces are useful for implementing multi-tenancy in a Kubernetes cluster. You can allocate separate Namespaces to different teams, projects, or users, providing isolation and resource control. This ensures that resources in one Namespace don't interfere with those in another.
2. **Resource Management:** Namespaces enable resource management and quota enforcement. You can define resource quotas (CPU, memory, storage) for each Namespace, preventing one Namespace from consuming all cluster resources and affecting others.
3. **Organization:** Namespaces help organize and categorize resources based on their purpose or ownership. For example, you might have a "development," "staging," and "production" Namespace for different environments or a "marketing" and "finance" Namespace for different departments.
4. **Security Boundaries:** Namespaces provide security boundaries by isolating resources. This is particularly important when dealing with sensitive data or applications, as you can enforce security policies at the Namespace level.
5. **Access Control:** Kubernetes Role-Based Access Control (RBAC) can be applied at the Namespace level, allowing you to control who has access to resources within a specific Namespace. This fine-grained access control enhances security.
6. **Resource Management:** Namespaces help in resource management by segregating resources based on project or team, making it easier to track and allocate resources efficiently.
7. **Testing and Development:** You can use Namespaces to create isolated environments for testing and development. This enables developers to work in a controlled environment without affecting the production system.
8. **Namespace Scoping:** When you use Kubernetes tools and commands, you can scope them to a specific Namespace. This means you can list, describe, or manage resources within a single Namespace without affecting resources in other Namespaces.

3 KUBERNETES ARCHITECTURE

Can you explain the key components of a Kubernetes cluster?

A Kubernetes cluster is composed of several key components that work together to manage and orchestrate containerized applications. Here are the primary components of a Kubernetes cluster:

1. **Master Node (Control Plane):**
   o **API Server:** The API server is the entry point for all administrative tasks in the cluster. It serves as the control plane's frontend, receiving and processing RESTful API requests from users, administrators, and controllers.
   o **etcd:** etcd is a distributed key-value store that stores the entire cluster's configuration data, including secrets, configuration settings, and the current state of the cluster. It provides a consistent and highly available data store.
   o **Controller Manager:** The controller manager is responsible for maintaining the desired state of the cluster by regulating and managing various controller processes. These controllers include the Node Controller, Replication Controller, and Endpoints Controller, among others.
   o **Scheduler:** The scheduler is responsible for placing Pods onto worker nodes based on resource requirements, affinity and anti-

affinity rules, and other constraints. It ensures optimal resource utilization and availability.

- o **Cloud Controller Manager (Optional):** In cloud environments, the cloud controller manager interfaces with the cloud provider's API to manage cloud-specific resources such as load balancers, persistent volumes, and virtual machines.

2. **Worker Nodes:**

- o **Kubelet:** The Kubelet is an agent running on each worker node. It communicates with the control plane and ensures that containers within Pods are running and healthy on the node. It takes care of starting, stopping, and monitoring containers.
- o **Container Runtime:** The container runtime, such as Docker or containerd, is responsible for running containers on worker nodes. It provides an environment where containers can be executed securely and efficiently.
- o **Kube Proxy:** Kube Proxy is responsible for network proxying and load balancing. It maintains network rules on the node to enable communication between Pods and external services, ensuring network connectivity.
- o **Pods:** Pods are the smallest deployable units in Kubernetes. They consist of one or more containers that share the same network namespace and can communicate with each other over localhost. Pods represent the unit of deployment and scaling.
- o **kubelet, container runtime, and kube proxy:** These components run on each worker node, collectively referred to as the "Node Components."

3. **Add-ons and Extensions (Optional):**

- o Kubernetes clusters often include additional add-ons and extensions to enhance functionality and ease of management. Examples include:
- ▪ **Dashboard:** A web-based user interface for cluster administration and monitoring.
- ▪ **Ingress Controller:** Manages external access to services within the cluster.
- ▪ **CNI Plugins:** Container Network Interface plugins for managing network configurations and policies.
- ▪ **Logging and Monitoring:** Tools like Prometheus and Grafana for monitoring cluster health and application performance.
- ▪ **DNS:** Provides DNS-based service discovery within the cluster.

4. **Networking:**
    o Kubernetes requires a networking solution that enables communication between Pods and external clients. Networking plugins, like Calico, Flannel, and Cilium, are used to implement network policies, pod-to-pod communication, and service discovery.
5. **Storage (Optional):**
    o Storage solutions and plugins are used to provide persistent storage to applications running in Pods. This includes storage classes, persistent volumes (PVs), and persistent volume claims (PVCs).
6. **Security and RBAC:**
    o Kubernetes includes Role-Based Access Control (RBAC) for defining and managing permissions within the cluster. Security features like PodSecurityPolicies and Network Policies enhance cluster security.
7. **Authentication and Authorization:**
    o Kubernetes can integrate with various authentication providers, such as OAuth, LDAP, or client certificates, to authenticate users and processes. Role-Based Access Control (RBAC) defines what actions they can perform based on their roles and permissions.

What is the role of the Master node in Kubernetes?

The Master node in a Kubernetes cluster plays a central and critical role in the management and orchestration of containerized applications. It is the brain of the Kubernetes cluster, responsible for controlling and coordinating all activities within the cluster. Here are the primary roles and responsibilities of the Master node:

1. **API Server:** The API server is the entry point for all REST commands used to control the cluster. It validates and processes incoming requests, then communicates with the etcd data store and other cluster components to perform the requested operations. Essentially, it serves as the control plane's front-end.

2. **etcd**: etcd is a distributed key-value store that stores the configuration data of the entire cluster. It is used to store the desired state of the cluster, including information about pods, services, and configurations. The Master nodes interact with etcd to read and write cluster state.

3. **Controller Manager**: The Controller Manager is responsible for ensuring that the desired state of the cluster matches the actual state. It includes various controllers that watch for changes in the cluster (e.g., replication controllers, deployment controllers) and take action to correct any deviations from the desired state.

4. **Scheduler**: The Scheduler is responsible for placing new pods onto nodes in the cluster. It takes into account factors like resource availability, node constraints, and affinity/anti-affinity rules to make intelligent placement decisions.

5. **Cloud Controller Manager (Optional)**: In cloud-based Kubernetes deployments, this component manages interactions with the underlying cloud provider's infrastructure. It enables features like load balancers, auto-scaling, and persistent storage integration with cloud-specific APIs.

6. **Addon Services**: Some Kubernetes distributions include additional components, such as DNS servers (like CoreDNS) and the Kubernetes Dashboard, which are typically deployed on the Master node to provide essential cluster services.

It's important to note that in production environments, it is common to have multiple Master nodes for high availability and fault tolerance. These Master nodes are often set up in an active-passive or active-active configuration to ensure that the control plane remains available even if one Master node fails.

What is the role of Worker nodes in a Kubernetes cluster?

Worker nodes, also known as minion nodes, form the worker or compute layer of a Kubernetes cluster. They are responsible for running containers and executing the workloads that make up your applications. Here are the key roles and responsibilities of Worker nodes in a Kubernetes cluster:

1. **Running Containers:** Worker nodes host and execute containers, which are encapsulated units containing application code, runtime, libraries, and dependencies. Containers run within Pods, and Worker nodes are responsible for managing these Pods.

2. **Kubelet (Node Agent):** Kubelet is an agent that runs on each Worker node. Its primary role is to ensure that containers within Pods are running and healthy. Kubelet communicates with the control plane (Master node) to receive instructions about which Pods to run and to report the status of those Pods.

3. **Container Runtime:** Worker nodes have a container runtime installed, such as Docker, containerd, or another compatible runtime. The container runtime is responsible for starting and managing containers based on container images.

4. **Kube Proxy:** Kube Proxy is a network proxy service that runs on each Worker node. It maintains network rules on the node to enable communication between Pods and external services. Kube Proxy facilitates load balancing and network routing for Pods.

5. **Pods:** Pods are the smallest deployable units in Kubernetes, and they run on Worker nodes. A Pod can contain one or more containers that share the same network namespace, storage volumes, and other resources. Worker nodes are responsible for creating and managing Pods.

6. **Networking:** Worker nodes are responsible for implementing the network connectivity and routing required for Pods to communicate with each other and with external services. Kubernetes Networking plugins, like Calico, Flannel, or Cilium, are used to set up networking configurations.

7. **Resource Isolation:** Worker nodes ensure resource isolation for containers. Each container runs within a Pod, and the node is responsible for isolating the resources (CPU, memory, filesystem) of each Pod from other Pods running on the same node.

8. **Monitoring and Logging:** Worker nodes generate logs and metrics related to container and node health. Monitoring and logging solutions can be used to collect and analyze this data for troubleshooting and performance analysis.

9. **Resource Utilization:** Worker nodes manage the allocation of CPU and memory resources to containers, ensuring that containers receive their requested resources and do not consume more than their specified limits.
10. **Autoscaling:** Worker nodes can be part of the cluster's autoscaling mechanism, where nodes are dynamically added or removed to meet resource demands. This helps maintain a balance between resource availability and workload requirements.
11. **Container Lifecycle:** Worker nodes handle the complete lifecycle of containers, including container startup, monitoring, scaling, and termination. They ensure that containers are in the desired state as defined by the Master node.

What is etcd, and why is it critical in Kubernetes?

etcd is a distributed key-value store that serves as the primary data store for Kubernetes. It is a critical and fundamental component of Kubernetes because it stores the entire configuration and state information of the cluster. Here's a closer look at what etcd is and why it is crucial in Kubernetes:

Key Characteristics of etcd:

1. **Consistency:** etcd provides strong consistency guarantees, ensuring that all reads and writes to the data store are globally ordered and appear to be executed instantaneously.
2. **Distributed:** It is designed to be distributed across multiple nodes, which enhances its fault tolerance and availability. Data is replicated across nodes, and etcd can automatically recover from failures.
3. **Watchable:** etcd supports watch operations, allowing clients to watch for changes to specific keys in real-time. This feature is crucial for triggering actions in response to changes in the cluster's configuration.

Why etcd is Critical in Kubernetes:

1. **Configuration Data Store:** etcd is used to store the entire configuration of a Kubernetes cluster, including information about nodes, pods, services, namespaces, deployments, and other resources. This configuration data is crucial for the cluster's operation.

2. **Desired State:** Kubernetes relies on etcd to maintain the desired state of the cluster. When you declare how you want your applications to run (e.g., the number of replicas, resource requirements), Kubernetes stores this desired state in etcd.

3. **Cluster State:** etcd keeps track of the current state of the cluster, including the actual state of resources, their current status, and their relationships. This allows Kubernetes to continuously monitor and reconcile the cluster's state with the desired state.

4. **High Availability:** etcd's distributed and replicated nature ensures high availability of cluster data. Even if some etcd nodes fail or experience issues, the cluster can continue to operate without data loss.

5. **Failure Recovery:** In the event of a failure or loss of data, etcd can recover by using the data stored on healthy nodes. This resilience ensures that the cluster can quickly return to a consistent state after issues are resolved.

6. **Cluster Scaling:** etcd can scale horizontally by adding more nodes to the etcd cluster. This scalability is essential as Kubernetes clusters grow to accommodate more workloads and nodes.

7. **Security:** etcd supports role-based access control (RBAC) and authentication mechanisms to secure access to cluster data. This helps protect the confidentiality and integrity of sensitive configuration information.

8. **Cluster Upgrades:** When performing Kubernetes cluster upgrades, etcd data is carefully migrated to maintain compatibility with the new Kubernetes version. This ensures that the cluster retains its configuration and state across upgrades.

9. **Backup and Restore:** Regular backups of etcd data are essential for disaster recovery and cluster migration scenarios. Kubernetes operators often implement backup strategies to protect the cluster's data.

How does Kubernetes ensure high availability?

Kubernetes is designed to ensure high availability (HA) for containerized applications and the platform itself. It achieves HA through a combination of architectural principles, redundancy, automated management, and fault tolerance mechanisms. Here's how Kubernetes ensures high availability:

1. **Master Node Redundancy:**
   - Kubernetes employs a multi-master architecture with multiple control plane nodes (Master nodes). This redundancy ensures that if one master node fails, others can take over, maintaining the control plane's availability.
   - An external load balancer or a virtual IP (VIP) can be used to distribute incoming requests among the control plane nodes. This load balancing further enhances the control plane's availability.
2. **etcd Cluster:**
   - etcd, the distributed key-value store used by Kubernetes, is typically deployed as a clustered system with multiple etcd nodes. This provides data redundancy and fault tolerance.
   - Data is replicated across etcd nodes, ensuring that even if some nodes fail, the cluster can continue to function without data loss.
3. **Node Redundancy:**
   - Worker nodes (minion nodes) are typically part of a pool of nodes. Kubernetes can automatically schedule Pods to available nodes, ensuring that if one node becomes unavailable, Pods can be rescheduled to other healthy nodes.
   - Cluster Autoscaler can be used to dynamically add or remove nodes based on resource demands, further enhancing worker node availability.
4. **Replication Controllers and StatefulSets:**
   - Replication Controllers and StatefulSets are used to manage the desired number of Pod replicas. If Pods fail or nodes become unavailable, these controllers automatically create replacement Pods on healthy nodes, ensuring the desired number of replicas is maintained.
5. **Self-Healing:**

o Kubernetes has built-in mechanisms for self-healing. If a Pod or container becomes unhealthy, the kubelet on the worker node detects this and can restart the container or reschedule the Pod to another node.

o Controller Managers continuously monitor the cluster's state and take corrective actions to ensure that the desired state is maintained.

6. **Rolling Updates:**
   o Kubernetes supports rolling updates of applications, allowing you to update application versions without downtime. This ensures that applications can be updated while remaining available to users.
   o Rolling updates gradually replace old Pods with new ones, verifying the health of each new Pod before proceeding.

7. **Service Discovery and Load Balancing:**
   o Kubernetes Services provide load balancing for Pods. Even if some Pods are scaled up or down, Services ensure that traffic is distributed to healthy Pods.
   o DNS-based service discovery allows clients to discover and access services by name, making it possible to route traffic to available Pods.

8. **Fault Tolerance Mechanisms:**
   o Kubernetes includes various fault tolerance mechanisms, such as node affinity and anti-affinity rules, Pod Disruption Budgets, and resource quotas, that help ensure application components are distributed and that resources are allocated appropriately.

9. **Backup and Disaster Recovery:**
   o Regular backups of etcd data, along with appropriate disaster recovery strategies, are crucial for protecting against data loss and ensuring cluster recovery in the event of a catastrophic failure.

10. **Security Measures:**
    o Kubernetes employs security features like Role-Based Access Control (RBAC) and network policies to protect the cluster from unauthorized access and potential security threats.

4 DEPLOYING APPLICATIONS

How can you deploy an application in Kubernetes?

Deploying an application in Kubernetes involves several steps and manifests to define the desired state of your application. Here's a high-level overview of the process:

1. **Create Container Images:** First, you need to containerize your application by creating Docker or container images. These images encapsulate your application code, runtime, libraries, and dependencies.
2. **Create Kubernetes Manifests:**
o   **Deployment Manifest:** Create a Kubernetes Deployment manifest. This defines how your application should run, including the number of replicas, container image, resource requirements, and more.

```
apiVersion: apps/v1
kind: Deployment
metadata:
  name: my-app-deployment
spec:
  replicas: 3
  selector:
    matchLabels:
```

```
      app: my-app
  template:
    metadata:
      labels:
        app: my-app
    spec:
      containers:
      - name: my-app-container
        image: your-registry/your-image:tag
        ports:
        - containerPort: 80
```

- **Service Manifest:** Optionally, create a Kubernetes Service manifest to expose your application to the network and provide load balancing. You can choose from various Service types, such as ClusterIP, NodePort, or LoadBalancer, depending on your requirements.

```
apiVersion: v1
kind: Service
metadata:
  name: my-app-service
spec:
  selector:
    app: my-app
  ports:
  - protocol: TCP
    port: 80
    targetPort: 80
  type: LoadBalancer
```

- **Apply Manifests:** Use the kubectl apply command to apply your Deployment and Service manifests to the Kubernetes cluster:

```
kubectl apply -f deployment.yaml
kubectl apply -f service.yaml
```

- **Monitoring and Scaling:**

- Monitor the status of your Pods and Deployments using kubectl get pods and kubectl get deployments.

- Use Kubernetes Horizontal Pod Autoscaling to automatically adjust the number of Pods based on resource utilization or custom metrics.
- Utilize Kubernetes tools or third-party monitoring solutions to gain insights into application performance.

• Update and Rollback:

- To update your application, modify the Deployment manifest (e.g., change the image version) and apply the changes using kubectl apply. Kubernetes will perform a rolling update to ensure minimal downtime.
- If an update introduces issues, you can rollback to a previous version by using kubectl rollout undo.

• Logging and Troubleshooting:

- Use Kubernetes logging solutions or third-party tools to collect and analyze application logs.
- Troubleshoot issues by inspecting Pod logs, examining resource utilization, and using debugging techniques.

• Secrets and Configurations:

- Store sensitive information and configuration data as Kubernetes Secrets and ConfigMaps. Inject these into your application containers as environment variables or mounted volumes.

• Continuous Integration/Continuous Deployment (CI/CD):

- Implement a CI/CD pipeline to automate the building and deployment of container images to a container registry. Use tools like Jenkins, GitLab CI/CD, or Tekton for this purpose.

• Application Lifecycle Management:

- Continuously manage the lifecycle of your application, including updates, scaling, backups, and disaster recovery strategies.

What is a Deployment in Kubernetes?

In Kubernetes, a **Deployment** is an API resource and a higher-level abstraction that allows you to define, manage, and control the rollout and scaling of your containerized applications. Deployments are a critical tool for ensuring the availability, reliability, and ease of updates for applications running in Kubernetes clusters. Here are the key features and purposes of Deployments:

1. **Declarative Updates:** Deployments enable you to specify the desired state of your application and its replicas. You declare how many replicas should run, which container image to use, and other configuration details in a declarative manner using a YAML manifest. Kubernetes then takes care of making the current state match the desired state.

2. **Rolling Updates:** Deployments support rolling updates, which allow you to update your application without downtime or service interruption. When you update the Deployment's Pod template (e.g., by changing the container image version), Kubernetes automatically manages the transition from the old version to the new one, ensuring that a certain number of Pods are available at all times.

3. **Rollback:** If an update introduces issues or unexpected behavior, Deployments provide a built-in mechanism for rolling back to a previous known-good state. This feature is crucial for maintaining application stability during updates.

4. **Scaling:** You can scale the number of replicas (Pods) up or down by simply modifying the desired replica count in the Deployment manifest. Kubernetes will automatically adjust the number of Pods to match the desired count, helping you handle changes in traffic and resource demands.

5. **Self-Healing:** Deployments monitor the health of Pods and replace failed Pods with new ones. If a Pod becomes unresponsive or crashes, the Deployment controller ensures that a replacement Pod is created to maintain the desired replica count.

6. **Replica Sets:** Under the hood, Deployments manage Replica Sets, which are responsible for maintaining a specified number of

Pods with a consistent configuration. Each Deployment creates and manages its associated Replica Set(s).

What is a StatefulSet, and when would you use it?

A **StatefulSet** is a Kubernetes resource that is used to manage stateful applications in a Kubernetes cluster. Unlike Deployments or ReplicaSets, which are well-suited for stateless workloads, StatefulSets are designed for applications that require stable and unique network identities, stable storage, and ordered, predictable scaling and rollout. StatefulSets are particularly valuable for deploying databases, distributed storage systems, and other stateful applications. Here's a closer look at what StatefulSets are and when you would use them:

Key Characteristics and Features of StatefulSets:

1. **Stable Network Identities:** Each Pod managed by a StatefulSet receives a stable and unique network identity (hostname) that persists across rescheduling and updates. This enables other Pods to reliably locate and communicate with individual Pods in the StatefulSet.
2. **Ordered Deployment:** StatefulSets ensure that Pods are deployed and scaled in a predictable, ordinal manner. Each Pod has an associated index that reflects its position in the StatefulSet. This ordering can be crucial for applications that rely on specific sequencing.
3. **Stable Storage:** StatefulSets can request and manage persistent storage volumes for Pods. This is essential for stateful applications that require data persistence, such as databases, caches, or distributed storage systems.
4. **Headless Services:** StatefulSets often pair with a headless Service (a service without a ClusterIP) to provide DNS-based service discovery for Pods. This allows other Pods to discover and connect to individual stateful Pods using their stable network identities.

When to Use StatefulSets:

You would use a StatefulSet in Kubernetes when:

1. **Stateful Applications:** Your application is stateful, meaning it maintains data or a state that must persist beyond the lifetime of an individual Pod.
2. **Stable Network Identities:** Your application requires stable network identities or hostnames that persist across rescheduling and updates. This is common in database clusters, where each node needs to be uniquely identifiable.
3. **Ordered Deployment:** Your application relies on a specific deployment order or sequencing, and Pods must be deployed and scaled in an ordered fashion.
4. **Persistent Storage:** Your stateful application requires persistent storage volumes, such as data directories or volumes, for data retention.
5. **Cluster Discovery:** You need to enable cluster discovery and communication among the members of your stateful application. Each Pod in a StatefulSet can be accessed by a predictable hostname and can discover others through DNS.
6. **Data Migration and Scaling:** You anticipate the need to perform data migration, scaling, or rolling updates in a controlled and predictable manner.

Common use cases for StatefulSets include deploying databases (e.g., MySQL, PostgreSQL, Cassandra), distributed file systems (e.g., NFS, Ceph), message queues (e.g., RabbitMQ, Kafka), and other stateful applications where data consistency and predictability are paramount.

How do you manage configuration and secrets in Kubernetes?

In Kubernetes, managing configuration and secrets is crucial for maintaining the security, flexibility, and portability of your containerized applications. Kubernetes provides dedicated resources and best practices for handling configuration data and sensitive information known as secrets. Here's how you can manage configuration and secrets effectively:

Configuration Management:

1. **ConfigMaps:** Kubernetes ConfigMaps are used to store configuration data in key-value pairs. ConfigMaps can be created from literal values, files, or directories, and they are designed to separate configuration from application code. Here's an example ConfigMap:

```
apiVersion: v1
kind: ConfigMap
metadata:
  name: my-config
data:
  key1: value1
  key2: value2
```

- To use ConfigMaps in a Pod, you can mount them as volumes or set environment variables. For example:

```
apiVersion: v1
kind: Pod
metadata:
  name: my-pod
spec:
  containers:
  - name: my-container
    image: my-image
    env:
    - name: KEY1
      valueFrom:
        configMapKeyRef:
          name: my-config
          key: key1
```

   o ConfigMaps are suitable for storing configuration files, environment variables, and any non-sensitive data that your application needs.
2. **External Configuration Stores:** For complex configuration management, you can use external configuration stores like Git repositories, databases, or specialized configuration management

tools (e.g., Helm). Kubernetes can pull configuration data from these sources during deployment.

Secrets Management:

1. **Secrets:** Kubernetes Secrets are used to store sensitive data such as passwords, API keys, and TLS certificates. Secrets are encoded and encrypted at rest in etcd, making them a secure way to manage sensitive information. Here's an example Secret:

```
apiVersion: v1
kind: Secret
metadata:
  name: my-secret
data:
  username: dXNlcm5hbWU=
  password: cGFzc3dvcmQ=
```

*   Secrets can be used in a similar way to ConfigMaps by mounting them as volumes or setting environment variables within Pods.

```
apiVersion: v1
kind: Pod
metadata:
  name: my-pod
spec:
  containers:
  - name: my-container
    image: my-image
    env:
    - name: DB_USERNAME
      valueFrom:
        secretKeyRef:
          name: my-secret
          key: username
```

*   **Secret Encryption:** Kubernetes allows you to encrypt sensitive data inside Secrets using the Kubernetes Key Management Service (KMS). This adds an additional layer of security to protect your secrets.

• **Service Accounts:** Kubernetes Service Accounts can be associated with Pods, and they grant permission to access Secrets. Use Service Accounts to control which Pods have access to specific Secrets.

• **Role-Based Access Control (RBAC):** RBAC policies can be used to control who can create, read, update, or delete Secrets within a cluster, adding an extra layer of access control.

• **External Vault or Key Management Systems:** For advanced secrets management and encryption, you can integrate Kubernetes with external Vault or Key Management Systems (KMS) to centralize secrets management, rotation, and access control.

Explain the concept of Helm in Kubernetes.

Helm is a package manager for Kubernetes that simplifies the process of defining, installing, and managing applications and their dependencies within a Kubernetes cluster. It serves as a bridge between the application definitions (charts) and the Kubernetes resources required to run those applications.

Here are the key concepts and components of Helm:

1. **Chart:** A Helm chart is a package containing all the resource definitions necessary to run a specific application in a Kubernetes cluster. Charts are organized into directories and contain metadata, templates, and optional values files. Charts can be shared and reused across different environments and clusters.
2. **Template:** Templates within a Helm chart are written in Go templating language and define Kubernetes resource manifests (YAML files). These templates can include placeholders (e.g., {{ .Values.image }}) that Helm substitutes with user-defined values during installation, making the charts highly configurable.
3. **Release:** When you install a Helm chart in a Kubernetes cluster, it creates an instance of that application called a "release." Each release has a unique name and can have different configurations, allowing multiple instances of the same application to coexist in the same cluster.

4. **Repository:** Helm charts can be stored in repositories, which are accessible over HTTP or other protocols. Helm repositories make it easy to share and distribute charts across teams and organizations.
5. **Values:** Values files contain user-configurable parameters that can be used to customize the behavior of Helm charts. These values can be overridden during installation, making it possible to adapt a chart to different environments or requirements without modifying the chart itself.

Here's a typical workflow for using Helm in Kubernetes:

1. **Create or Obtain a Chart:** You can create your own Helm chart for your application or obtain pre-built charts from Helm repositories. Helm Hub is a popular public repository for Helm charts.
2. **Customize Values:** Modify the values in the values.yaml file or create your own values file to customize the configuration of the chart according to your requirements. These values will be used to fill in the placeholders in the chart templates.
3. **Install the Chart:** Use the helm install command to install a Helm chart into your Kubernetes cluster, specifying the chart name and any custom values files you want to use.
4. **Upgrade and Rollback:** Helm provides commands for upgrading an existing release to a new version or rolling back to a previous release if an update causes issues.
5. **List and Manage Releases:** You can list the releases in your cluster, query release status, and delete releases when they are no longer needed.
6. **Helm Plugins:** Helm supports plugins that can extend its functionality. You can install and use Helm plugins to add features like linting, testing, or repository management.

Helm simplifies the deployment and management of complex applications in Kubernetes by providing a standardized way to package and configure them. It reduces the complexity of managing Kubernetes manifests and encourages best practices for application packaging and versioning. Helm has become a fundamental tool in the Kubernetes ecosystem for both application developers and cluster administrators.

5 NETWORKING IN KUBERNETES

What is the Kubernetes Service Discovery mechanism?

Kubernetes Service Discovery is a crucial mechanism that allows Pods within a Kubernetes cluster to discover and communicate with other services or Pods. It ensures that applications can locate and interact with the various components of a distributed system without hardcoding IP addresses or hostnames. Kubernetes provides several ways to achieve service discovery:

1. **DNS-Based Service Discovery:**
   - Kubernetes assigns a DNS name to each Service in the cluster. The DNS name is based on the Service's name and namespace, following the format: <service-name>.<namespace>.svc.cluster.local.
   - Pods within the cluster can use this DNS name to resolve the IP addresses of Services. For example, if you have a Service named my-service in the my-namespace namespace, other Pods can access it using my-service.my-namespace.svc.cluster.local.
   - DNS-based service discovery is the most common and convenient way for Pods to locate and connect to Services.
2. **Environment Variables:**

o Kubernetes automatically sets environment variables for each Service within a Pod. These variables are in the format <SERVICE_NAME>_SERVICE_HOST and <SERVICE_NAME>_SERVICE_PORT_<PORT_NAME>. For example, if you have a Service named my-service, you can access its host and port using MY_SERVICE_SERVICE_HOST and MY_SERVICE_SERVICE_PORT.

3. **Service Names and Labels:**
   o Kubernetes also allows you to use Service names and labels to discover Services. You can query the Kubernetes API to obtain information about Services, including their IP addresses and ports. This approach is less commonly used than DNS-based service discovery but provides programmatic access to Service information.

4. **Ingress Controllers:**
   o Ingress controllers, which manage external access to Services, often use hostnames and path-based routing for service discovery. Ingress resources define routing rules, allowing external clients to access different Services based on the requested hostname or URL path.

Service discovery is fundamental for building scalable and resilient applications in Kubernetes. It abstracts the underlying network complexities and allows developers to focus on designing their applications in a more decoupled and portable way. Whether you're building microservices, deploying databases, or setting up communication between various components of your application, Kubernetes Service Discovery ensures that your services can find and communicate with each other reliably and flexibly.

How does Ingress work in Kubernetes?

In Kubernetes, **Ingress** is a resource and a controller that manages external access to services within a cluster. It serves as an API object that defines rules for routing external HTTP and HTTPS traffic to different services and Pods based on hostnames or URL paths. Ingress controllers, such as Nginx Ingress Controller or Traefik, implement these rules by configuring external load balancers or reverse proxies to handle the traffic.

Here's how Ingress works in Kubernetes:

1. **Ingress Resource Definition:**
   - You create an Ingress resource by defining a YAML manifest that specifies the rules for routing traffic. An Ingress resource typically includes the following:
     - Hostnames (optional): You can specify one or more hostnames for which the Ingress rules apply. For example, you can define rules for app.example.com and api.example.com.
     - Paths (optional): You can define URL paths to route traffic to different services. For example, you can route /app to one service and /api to another.
   - Backend services: You specify the backend services (usually Kubernetes Services) that should receive the traffic. Each rule maps to a particular backend service.

   ### Here's a simplified example of an Ingress resource definition:

```
apiVersion: networking.k8s.io/v1
kind: Ingress
metadata:
  name: my-ingress
spec:
  rules:
    - host: app.example.com
      http:
        paths:
          - path: /
            pathType: Prefix
            backend:
              service:
                name: app-service
                port:
                  number: 80
    - host: api.example.com
      http:
```

```
paths:
  - path: /api
    pathType: Prefix
    backend:
      service:
        name: api-service
        port:
          number: 8080
```

• **Ingress Controller:**

• An Ingress controller is a component responsible for implementing the rules defined in Ingress resources. Kubernetes allows multiple Ingress controllers to coexist in a cluster, each potentially serving different purposes or routing to different external resources.

• The Ingress controller watches for changes in Ingress resources. When a new Ingress resource is created or updated, the controller configures external load balancers, reverse proxies, or other routing mechanisms to apply the specified rules.

• **External Access:**

• External traffic (e.g., from the internet) is directed to the cluster's external load balancer or ingress controller. The ingress controller inspects the incoming requests and applies the routing rules defined in the Ingress resource.

• **Routing and Load Balancing:**

• Based on the hostname and URL path, the Ingress controller routes incoming requests to the appropriate backend services and Pods within the cluster. Load balancing may also be applied if multiple Pods serve the same service.

• **SSL Termination (Optional):**

• Ingress controllers can also manage SSL/TLS termination, allowing you to secure external traffic by applying SSL certificates to specific hostnames or routes. This is achieved by configuring the ingress controller with the necessary certificates.

- **HTTP/HTTPS Traffic:**

- Ingress resources can be configured to handle both HTTP and HTTPS traffic. For HTTPS, you typically need to specify a Secret containing SSL/TLS certificates and configure the Ingress to use that Secret for SSL termination.

What are Network Policies, and why are they important in Kubernetes?

Network Policies in Kubernetes are a resource type that allow you to define and enforce rules for network communication between Pods. They act as a crucial layer of security and isolation within a Kubernetes cluster, providing fine-grained control over which Pods are allowed to communicate with each other and on which network ports.

Here's why Network Policies are important in Kubernetes:

1. **Security:** Network Policies enhance the security of your Kubernetes cluster by allowing you to define explicit rules governing network traffic. By default, all Pods can communicate with each other within the cluster, which may not be desirable, especially in multi-tenant or production environments. Network Policies enable you to lock down communication and implement the principle of least privilege.
2. **Isolation:** In a multi-tenant environment, different teams or applications may run on the same cluster. Network Policies allow you to isolate Pods and services, preventing unintended communication between them. This isolation prevents one compromised or misconfigured Pod from affecting others.
3. **Compliance:** In regulated industries or environments with strict compliance requirements, Network Policies help ensure that communication adheres to specific compliance standards. For

example, you can define policies to enforce data residency or data protection regulations.

4. **Microservices Architecture:** In microservices architectures, where applications are composed of many small, interacting services, controlling network traffic becomes critical. Network Policies allow you to specify which services can communicate, helping you maintain a well-structured and secure microservices network.

5. **Defense in Depth:** Network Policies complement other security mechanisms in Kubernetes, such as Role-Based Access Control (RBAC) and Pod Security Policies. Together, these security layers provide a robust defense-in-depth strategy to protect your applications and data.

6. **Troubleshooting:** Network Policies can also aid in troubleshooting network-related issues. By examining the network policies applied to a particular Pod or service, you can gain insights into why certain connections are allowed or denied.

Here's a simplified example of a Network Policy:

```
apiVersion: networking.k8s.io/v1
kind: NetworkPolicy
metadata:
  name: deny-egress
spec:
  podSelector: {}
  policyTypes:
    - Egress
  egress:
    - ports:
        - protocol: TCP
          port: 80
```

In this example, the Network Policy denies all egress (outgoing) traffic from all Pods in the cluster on port 80. This is a simple illustration, but you can create more complex policies to specify source and destination Pods, IP blocks, and ports.

Overall, Network Policies are a critical tool for enhancing security, enforcing compliance, and maintaining isolation in Kubernetes clusters. They provide granular control over network traffic, allowing you to define who can communicate with whom and on which network ports, ultimately ensuring the integrity and security of your applications and data.

What is a CNI (Container Network Interface), and how does it relate to Kubernetes?

A **Container Network Interface (CNI)** is a standardized specification and set of libraries that define how network plugins interact with container runtimes like Docker and container orchestration systems like Kubernetes. CNIs are essential for configuring networking for containers and Pods within a Kubernetes cluster.

Here's how CNIs relate to Kubernetes:

1. **Network Plugin Integration:** In Kubernetes, Pods are the smallest deployable units, and they often consist of one or more containers that need to communicate with each other and with external services. CNIs provide a standardized way for Kubernetes to delegate network configuration tasks to network plugins.
2. **Flexibility:** Kubernetes supports various network plugins, and CNIs ensure that these plugins can be seamlessly integrated with the container runtime and the Kubernetes control plane. This flexibility allows you to choose the most appropriate network plugin for your cluster's networking requirements.
3. **Container-to-Container Communication:** CNIs enable container-to-container communication within Pods. They configure network namespaces, bridges, and routing tables to ensure that containers within the same Pod can communicate with each other over the Pod's network namespace.
4. **Pod-to-Pod Communication:** CNIs also handle Pod-to-Pod communication. They set up network routing and policies to ensure that Pods can communicate with other Pods in the same cluster, either within the same node or across nodes in a multi-node cluster.

5. **External Connectivity:** CNIs configure network connectivity to external services and resources, including external networks, services hosted outside the cluster, and the internet. They often provide network address translation (NAT) and routing capabilities to enable Pods to access external resources.

6. **Security and Isolation:** CNIs can enforce network policies and isolation between Pods using technologies like network namespaces, firewall rules, and virtual LAN (VLAN) segmentation. This helps in implementing security and isolation requirements for applications.

Popular CNI plugins in the Kubernetes ecosystem include Calico, Flannel, Weave, Cilium, and more. Each of these plugins may offer different networking features, performance characteristics, and security capabilities, allowing you to choose the one that best suits your use case.

6 STORAGE IN KUBERNETES

How does Kubernetes handle storage for containers?

Kubernetes provides several mechanisms for handling storage for containers, allowing you to manage both ephemeral and persistent storage requirements. Here's how Kubernetes handles storage for containers:

1. **Ephemeral Storage**:
   o **EmptyDir Volumes:** Kubernetes allows you to create ephemeral storage volumes using EmptyDir volumes. These volumes are created when a Pod is scheduled on a node and are deleted when the Pod is removed or rescheduled elsewhere. They are typically used for temporary storage needs within a single Pod.
   o **Projected Volumes:** Projected volumes allow you to combine different data sources, such as Secret, ConfigMap, and downward API, into a single volume. These volumes are also ephemeral and can be useful for exposing configuration files or secrets to your Pods.
   o **HostPath Volumes:** HostPath volumes allow Pods to use a directory on the node's filesystem as storage. While these volumes can be used for persistent storage, they are typically used for ephemeral data as well.

2. **Persistent Storage:**
o **Persistent Volumes (PVs) and Persistent Volume Claims (PVCs):** Kubernetes introduces the concept of Persistent Volumes (PVs) and Persistent Volume Claims (PVCs) to manage persistent storage. PVs are cluster-level resources that represent physical storage, while PVCs are requests for storage by Pods. PVCs can dynamically bind to available PVs or be statically bound to specific PVs.
o **Storage Classes:** Storage Classes define the characteristics of PVs and provide a way to dynamically provision storage based on class definitions. For example, you can define different Storage Classes that use different types of storage devices or providers (e.g., AWS EBS, Azure Disk, CSI-compliant storage systems).
o **Volume Modes:** Kubernetes supports two volume modes: Filesystem and Block. Filesystem mode is the default and is used for most cases where a filesystem is required. Block mode is used for scenarios where raw block storage is needed, such as databases that want to manage their own filesystem.
o **Access Modes:** PVs and PVCs support different access modes: ReadWriteOnce (RWO), ReadOnlyMany (ROX), and ReadWriteMany (RWX). These modes determine whether the storage can be mounted as read-write by a single Pod (RWO), read-only by multiple Pods (ROX), or read-write by multiple Pods (RWX).
3. **CSI (Container Storage Interface):** Kubernetes introduces CSI as an extensible standard for container orchestration platforms to interact with storage providers. CSI drivers enable storage vendors to develop plugins that can be easily integrated into Kubernetes clusters. This extensibility allows for more diverse and specialized storage solutions to be used with Kubernetes.
4. **StatefulSets:** When dealing with stateful applications like databases, Kubernetes offers StatefulSets. StatefulSets provide guarantees about the ordering and uniqueness of Pods, which is essential for maintaining data consistency. Each Pod in a StatefulSet receives a stable network identity and persistent storage.
5. **Dynamic Provisioning:** Kubernetes can dynamically provision storage resources using Storage Classes. When a PVC is created, it can request storage from a specific Storage Class, and

Kubernetes will automatically provision the requested storage based on the class's configuration.

6. **Volume Expansion:** Kubernetes allows for volume expansion, enabling you to resize persistent volumes dynamically when your application's storage needs grow.

What is Persistent Volume (PV) and Persistent Volume Claim (PVC) in Kubernetes?

In Kubernetes, **Persistent Volume (PV)** and **Persistent Volume Claim (PVC)** are resources that enable the management of persistent storage in a cluster. They provide a way to abstract and separate the details of storage provisioning from the Pod definitions, allowing for greater flexibility and portability of storage configurations.

Here's an explanation of PVs and PVCs:

Persistent Volume (PV):

A Persistent Volume (PV) in Kubernetes represents a piece of physical storage in the cluster. PVs are cluster-level resources and are not associated with any specific Pod. They are created and managed by cluster administrators and provide a pool of storage resources that Pods can request.

Key characteristics of PVs:

1. **Provisioning:** PVs can be provisioned statically (pre-created by administrators) or dynamically (created on-demand using Storage Classes).
2. **Access Modes:** PVs support different access modes, such as ReadWriteOnce (RWO), ReadOnlyMany (ROX), and ReadWriteMany (RWX), which define how the storage can be accessed by Pods.
3. **Capacity:** PVs have a defined storage capacity, specifying the amount of storage available for use by Pods.

4. **Reclaim Policy:** PVs have a reclaim policy that determines what happens to the underlying storage when a PV is released. The reclaim policies include Retain (manual cleanup), Delete (automatic deletion), and Recycle (limited support).
5. **Storage Class Binding:** PVs can be associated with a Storage Class, allowing dynamic provisioning based on class definitions.
6. **Access Modes:** PVs can be associated with access modes (RWO, ROX, RWX) that specify how the storage can be accessed by Pods.

Persistent Volume Claim (PVC):

A Persistent Volume Claim (PVC) is a request for storage by a Pod. PVCs are created by developers or administrators when defining a Pod that requires persistent storage. When a PVC is created, it specifies requirements such as the desired storage capacity and access mode. Kubernetes then attempts to find an available PV that satisfies these requirements and binds the PVC to the PV.

Key characteristics of PVCs:

1. **Request for Storage:** PVCs request storage resources with specific capacity and access mode requirements.
2. **Binding to PV:** Kubernetes attempts to find a suitable PV that meets the PVC's requirements. The PVC is bound to the selected PV.
3. **Pod Consumption:** Once a PVC is bound to a PV, a Pod can use the PVC as a volume in its Pod specification. The Pod references the PVC, which, in turn, references the underlying PV.
4. **Dynamic Provisioning:** PVCs can dynamically provision storage based on the requirements specified in the PVC and the availability of PVs. This allows for on-demand storage allocation.

Explain the difference between StatefulSets and Deployments regarding storage.

StatefulSets and **Deployments** are both controller objects in Kubernetes used for managing Pods, but they differ significantly in how they handle storage, particularly for stateful applications:

Deployments:

1. **Statelessness:** Deployments are primarily designed for managing stateless applications. They are suitable for applications where individual Pods are interchangeable and don't require persistent storage. Deployments can easily scale up or down, and Pods can be replaced without concerns about data persistence.
2. **Pod Lifecycle:** Deployments manage Pods in a stateless manner. When scaling or updating a Deployment, existing Pods are terminated, and new Pods are created in their place. This means that data is not preserved across Pod rescheduling, as each Pod is considered disposable.
3. **Storage Volume:** While Deployments can use Volumes for temporary storage within a Pod's lifecycle, they don't inherently provide support for persistent storage across Pod replacements. If you need persistent storage for a stateless application managed by a Deployment, you would typically use a Persistent Volume (PV) and a Persistent Volume Claim (PVC) within the Pod's specification.

StatefulSets:

1. **Stateful Applications:** StatefulSets are designed explicitly for stateful applications, such as databases, message queues, or distributed storage systems, where each Pod has a unique identity and data persistence is critical.
2. **Stable Network Identity:** StatefulSets provide a stable network identity (hostname) and persistent storage for each Pod. Pods in a StatefulSet are created sequentially, and each Pod gets a unique hostname based on its ordinal index (e.g., web-0, web-1, etc.).
3. **Ordered Scaling:** Scaling a StatefulSet typically occurs in an ordered fashion. Pods are created and deleted sequentially to

maintain the desired order and prevent data loss. This ensures that data is not lost when Pods are replaced.

4. **Persistent Storage:** StatefulSets are inherently aware of persistent storage. They can automatically manage the lifecycle of persistent volumes associated with each Pod, ensuring that data is retained when Pods are rescheduled or updated. This is especially useful for databases where each Pod has its dedicated storage.

How can you provision dynamic storage in Kubernetes?

Provisioning dynamic storage in Kubernetes is accomplished by using Kubernetes Storage Classes and Persistent Volume Claims (PVCs). Dynamic storage provisioning allows you to create and allocate storage resources on-demand based on the characteristics specified in the PVC. Here's a step-by-step guide on how to provision dynamic storage:

1. **Define a Storage Class**:

    Start by defining a Storage Class. A Storage Class is a resource that describes the properties of the storage you want to provision. It includes information such as the type of storage, the provisioner to use (e.g., a cloud provider's storage service or a CSI driver), and any additional parameters.

    Here's an example of a Storage Class definition:

```
apiVersion: storage.k8s.io/v1
kind: StorageClass
metadata:
  name: my-storage-class
provisioner: my-provisioner
parameters:
  type: fast
```

In this example, "my-storage-class" is the name of the Storage Class, "my-provisioner" is the provisioner, and "type: fast" is a parameter specific to the provisioner.

- **Create a Persistent Volume Claim (PVC):**

Next, create a PVC that references the Storage Class. The PVC specifies the requirements for storage, such as capacity, access mode, and the Storage Class to use.

Example PVC definition:

```
apiVersion: v1
kind: PersistentVolumeClaim
metadata:
  name: my-pvc
spec:
  accessModes:
    - ReadWriteOnce
  resources:
    requests:
      storage: 10Gi
  storageClassName: my-storage-class
```

In this example, "my-pvc" is the name of the PVC, "ReadWriteOnce" is the access mode (indicating that the storage can be mounted as read-write by a single Pod), and "my-storage-class" is the Storage Class to use.

- **Apply the PVC to a Pod:**

Now, you can create a Pod that uses the PVC as a volume in its specification. The Pod will automatically request storage from the cluster based on the PVC definition. Here's a simplified Pod example:

```
apiVersion: v1
kind: Pod
metadata:
  name: my-pod
spec:
  volumes:
    - name: my-volume
```

```
    persistentVolumeClaim:
        claimName: my-pvc
  containers:
    - name: my-container
      image: nginx
      volumeMounts:
        - mountPath: /data
          name: my-volume
```

In this example, the Pod "my-pod" uses the PVC "my-pvc" as a volume named "my-volume." The volume is mounted at "/data" within the container.

- **Apply the YAML Manifests**:

Apply the Storage Class, PVC, and Pod YAML manifests to your Kubernetes cluster using the kubectl apply -f command:

```
kubectl apply -f storage-class.yaml
kubectl apply -f pvc.yaml
kubectl apply -f pod.yaml
```

Kubernetes will automatically handle the provisioning of storage based on the PVC's definition and the available Storage Class. The provisioned storage will be associated with the PVC and mounted into the Pod, making it available for use by your application.

Dynamic storage provisioning simplifies the management of storage resources in Kubernetes, ensuring that Pods have the required storage without manual intervention. This approach is especially valuable in dynamic, scalable environments where storage needs can change rapidly.

7 MONITORING AND LOGGING

What tools are commonly used for monitoring Kubernetes clusters?

Monitoring Kubernetes clusters effectively requires a combination of tools and solutions that can capture, store, analyze, and visualize data from various sources within the cluster. Here are some commonly used tools for monitoring Kubernetes clusters:

1. **Prometheus:**
   o Prometheus is an open-source monitoring system designed for reliability and scalability. It is highly popular in the Kubernetes ecosystem and excels at collecting and storing time-series data, including metrics from Kubernetes components, applications, and custom sources.
2. **Grafana:**
   o Grafana is a widely used open-source platform for creating and sharing dashboards and visualizations. It integrates seamlessly with Prometheus and other data sources, making it an excellent choice for building custom monitoring dashboards.
3. **Kubernetes Metrics Server:**
   o The Kubernetes Metrics Server is an essential component for collecting resource utilization metrics from your cluster, such

as CPU and memory usage. It enables the Horizontal Pod Autoscaler and provides valuable insights into node and Pod performance.

4. **Prometheus Operator:**
   o The Prometheus Operator simplifies the deployment and management of Prometheus instances in Kubernetes. It automates tasks like configuration, scaling, and service discovery, making Prometheus easier to set up and maintain.

5. **kube-state-metrics:**
   o kube-state-metrics is a service that collects metrics about the state of various Kubernetes objects, such as Pods, Services, and Deployments. These metrics provide insights into the health and status of your applications.

6. **Alertmanager:**
   o The Prometheus Alertmanager handles alerting and notification based on alerts generated by Prometheus. It allows you to define alerting rules and configure how and when notifications are sent, helping you proactively respond to issues.

7. **Elasticsearch, Fluentd, and Kibana (EFK Stack):**
   o The EFK stack is used for log aggregation and analysis. Elasticsearch stores and indexes logs, Fluentd collects and forwards logs to Elasticsearch, and Kibana provides a user-friendly interface for searching and visualizing log data.

8. **Jaeger and OpenTelemetry:**
   o For distributed tracing, Jaeger is a popular choice. It helps you understand how requests flow through your microservices. OpenTelemetry is an open-source project that provides libraries and agents for collecting distributed traces and metrics.

9. **Container Orchestration Tools:**
   o Kubernetes itself provides built-in monitoring capabilities through its components like kubelet, kube-proxy, and cAdvisor. These components expose metrics that can be collected and used for cluster-level monitoring.

10. **Custom Metrics and Logging Solutions:**
   o Depending on your specific requirements, you might choose to integrate custom monitoring and logging solutions. Some

organizations use commercial tools or managed services for more advanced observability.

11. **Cloud-Specific Monitoring Solutions:**
    o Cloud providers often offer their own Kubernetes monitoring solutions, such as AWS CloudWatch for Amazon EKS or Google Cloud Monitoring for Google Kubernetes Engine (GKE). These services can be seamlessly integrated with your cloud-managed Kubernetes clusters.

12. **Third-party Monitoring Platforms:**
    o There are several third-party monitoring platforms and solutions that offer comprehensive Kubernetes monitoring and alerting capabilities. These platforms provide features like anomaly detection, root cause analysis, and extensive integrations.

Selecting the right combination of monitoring tools depends on your specific requirements, existing infrastructure, and the level of observability you need for your Kubernetes clusters and applications. Many organizations opt for a combination of open-source tools and commercial solutions to meet their monitoring and observability needs effectively.

How can you collect and analyze logs in Kubernetes?

Collecting and analyzing logs in Kubernetes involves setting up a log aggregation system to gather logs from various sources within the cluster, centralize them for storage and analysis, and use visualization tools to gain insights. Here's a step-by-step guide on how to collect and analyze logs in Kubernetes:

Step 1: Choose a Logging Solution:

Select a logging solution that suits your needs. Common choices for log aggregation in Kubernetes include the Elastic Stack (EFK), Fluentd, and Loki. Each has its strengths and use cases.

Step 2: Deploy a Logging Agent:

Deploy a logging agent like Fluentd, Fluent Bit, or Filebeat as a DaemonSet on each node in your Kubernetes cluster. These agents are responsible for collecting log data from various sources, such as application Pods, system components, and containers.

Here's an example of a Fluentd DaemonSet configuration:

```
apiVersion: apps/v1
kind: DaemonSet
metadata:
  name: fluentd
  namespace: kube-system
spec:
  selector:
    matchLabels:
      app: fluentd-logging
  template:
    metadata:
      labels:
        app: fluentd-logging
    spec:
      containers:
        - name: fluentd
          image: fluent/fluentd:v1.12-debian
          resources:
            limits:
              memory: "500Mi"
            requests:
              cpu: "100m"
              memory: "200Mi"
          volumeMounts:
            - name: varlog
              mountPath: /var/log
            - name: varlibdockercontainers
              mountPath: /var/lib/docker/containers
      volumes:
        - name: varlog
          hostPath:
            path: /var/log
        - name: varlibdockercontainers
          hostPath:
            path: /var/lib/docker/containers
```

Step 3: Configure Application Logging:

Ensure that your applications are configured to send logs to stdout or stderr. Kubernetes will capture these logs, making them available for collection by the logging agent.

Step 4: Deploy the Logging Solution:

Deploy the chosen logging solution in your cluster. For example, if you are using the EFK stack (Elasticsearch, Fluentd, Kibana), you would deploy Elasticsearch for log storage, Fluentd for log collection, and Kibana for log visualization.

Step 5: Configure Fluentd or Logging Agent:

Configure the Fluentd or logging agent to forward collected logs to the central log storage (e.g., Elasticsearch). You may need to specify the Elasticsearch endpoint and authentication credentials in the Fluentd configuration.

Step 6: Visualize Logs:

Use visualization tools like Kibana, Grafana, or the log visualization features provided by your logging solution to create dashboards and queries for log analysis. These tools allow you to search, filter, and visualize log data to gain insights into your cluster's health and troubleshoot issues.

Step 7: Set Up Alerts and Notifications:

Implement alerting and notification mechanisms based on log data. You can use tools like Prometheus Alertmanager or built-in alerting features in your log visualization tool to set up alerts for specific log patterns or anomalies.

Step 8: Maintain and Optimize:

Regularly monitor and maintain your logging infrastructure. Ensure that log storage doesn't fill up, and configure log retention policies to manage log data effectively. Optimize queries and dashboards for efficient log analysis.

Step 9: Integrate with Other Observability Tools:

Consider integrating log data with other observability data sources, such as metrics and traces, to gain a holistic view of your Kubernetes applications. Tools like Jaeger and OpenTelemetry can assist with distributed tracing.

By following these steps, you can effectively collect, store, and analyze logs in your Kubernetes cluster, enabling you to monitor application performance, troubleshoot issues, and maintain the health and security of your containerized workloads.

What is Prometheus, and how does it work with Kubernetes?

Prometheus is an open-source monitoring and alerting system designed for reliability, scalability, and a focus on the simplicity of metrics and alerting. It is a popular choice for monitoring Kubernetes clusters and applications running within them. Prometheus follows a pull-based model for collecting and querying metrics, making it well-suited for dynamic and containerized environments like Kubernetes.

Here's how Prometheus works with Kubernetes:

1. **Data Collection and Exporters:**

    Prometheus collects metrics from various sources, including Kubernetes components, applications, and custom instrumentation. In Kubernetes, this is typically done using Prometheus exporters. Exporters are specialized applications that expose metrics in a format that Prometheus can scrape. Common exporters in the Kubernetes ecosystem include the `node_exporter` for node-level metrics and the `kube-state-metrics` for cluster state metrics.

2. **Configuration:**

   Prometheus is configured through YAML files that specify which targets (endpoints) to scrape for metrics. In a Kubernetes environment, you create a Prometheus configuration that includes the service endpoints of the exporters and other relevant targets. Kubernetes ConfigMaps or Helm charts are often used to manage the Prometheus configuration.

3. **Scraping and Storage:**

   Prometheus periodically scrapes metrics from the configured targets. It uses the data exposed by exporters and stores the collected time-series data in its local storage engine. Prometheus uses a pull-based approach, where it actively queries the targets based on the configured scrape interval.

4. **Query Language and PromQL:**

   Prometheus provides a powerful query language called PromQL (Prometheus Query Language) that allows you to query and aggregate metrics. You can create custom queries to gain insights into your Kubernetes cluster's performance, application behavior, and resource utilization.

5. **Alerting Rules:**

   Prometheus supports alerting rules, which enable you to define conditions and thresholds for generating alerts based on metric data. You can configure alerting rules to notify you when certain conditions are met, such as high CPU utilization or low available memory in your cluster.

6. **Grafana Integration:**

   While Prometheus provides a basic web interface for querying metrics and monitoring alerts, it is often used in conjunction with visualization tools like Grafana. Grafana allows you to create custom dashboards and visualize Prometheus metrics in a more user-friendly way. It also provides features for building alerting panels and creating comprehensive monitoring dashboards.

7. **Service Discovery:**

   In Kubernetes, Prometheus can take advantage of service discovery mechanisms to dynamically discover and monitor new Pods and services as they are deployed or scaled. Kubernetes-native service discovery ensures that Prometheus remains aware of changes in the cluster's topology.

8. **Horizontal Pod Autoscaling (HPA):**

   Prometheus metrics can be used as a data source for Kubernetes Horizontal Pod Autoscaling (HPA). HPA can automatically scale the number of Pods based on custom Prometheus metrics, helping you maintain optimal resource utilization and application performance.

Prometheus is highly customizable and adaptable to various monitoring needs. It provides a robust foundation for monitoring the health, performance, and availability of your Kubernetes applications and infrastructure. When combined with other observability tools, Prometheus can help you gain comprehensive insights into your Kubernetes ecosystem.

Explain the importance of the Kubernetes Dashboard.

The **Kubernetes Dashboard** is a web-based user interface that provides a graphical representation and management console for Kubernetes clusters. While Kubernetes can be managed entirely through command-line tools, the Kubernetes Dashboard offers several important benefits, making it a valuable tool for administrators, developers, and operators:

1. **Visual Representation:** The Kubernetes Dashboard provides a visual representation of your cluster's resources, making it easier to understand the overall state of your cluster. You can view information about Nodes, Pods, Services, Deployments, ConfigMaps, and more in a user-friendly format.

2. **Efficient Monitoring:** It offers a convenient way to monitor the health and status of your cluster components and applications. You can quickly check the status of Pods, Services, and Nodes, and identify any issues or failures without having to run multiple command-line queries.

3. **Resource Management:** Administrators can use the Dashboard to manage cluster resources, including creating, updating, and deleting Deployments, Services, ConfigMaps, and other Kubernetes objects. This simplifies resource management tasks for those who may not be familiar with Kubernetes YAML manifests.

4. **Troubleshooting:** Developers and operators can use the Dashboard to troubleshoot issues within the cluster. You can view logs and events for individual Pods, inspect resource utilization metrics, and gain insights into what might be causing problems.

5. **Security and Access Control:** The Kubernetes Dashboard supports integration with Kubernetes RBAC (Role-Based Access Control), allowing you to define granular access permissions for users and teams. This helps ensure that only authorized personnel can access and modify cluster resources.

6. **Access from Anywhere:** The Dashboard is accessible via a web browser, which means you can manage your Kubernetes cluster

from anywhere with network access to the cluster. This flexibility is especially useful for remote administration and monitoring.

7. **Resource Overview:** The Overview page in the Dashboard provides a high-level summary of the cluster's health and resource utilization, including CPU and memory usage, the number of running Pods, and other critical metrics.

8. **YAML Editing and Deployment:** The Dashboard includes a YAML editor that allows you to create, edit, and apply Kubernetes resource definitions directly. This is helpful for users who are learning Kubernetes or prefer a graphical interface for resource configuration.

9. **Extensibility:** The Dashboard is extensible and supports custom plugins and extensions. You can integrate additional features and views into the Dashboard to tailor it to your specific use cases.

10. **Learning and Training:** The Kubernetes Dashboard can serve as an educational tool for learning Kubernetes concepts and best practices. It provides an intuitive interface for exploring and interacting with Kubernetes resources.

While the Kubernetes Dashboard is a valuable tool, it's essential to ensure that it is properly secured and only accessible by authorized users. Proper RBAC and network access controls should be in place to protect sensitive cluster information. When configured and used correctly, the Kubernetes Dashboard can simplify cluster management, enhance monitoring and troubleshooting capabilities, and improve the overall Kubernetes experience for both beginners and experienced users.

8 SCALING AND LOAD BALANCING

How does Kubernetes auto-scaling work?

Kubernetes auto-scaling allows you to automatically adjust the number of Pods in a Deployment, ReplicaSet, or StatefulSet based on resource utilization metrics or custom criteria. It's a crucial feature for ensuring that your applications can efficiently handle varying levels of traffic without manual intervention. Here's how Kubernetes auto-scaling works:

1. **Horizontal Pod Autoscaler (HPA):** The primary resource responsible for auto-scaling in Kubernetes is the **Horizontal Pod Autoscaler (HPA)**. An HPA continuously monitors the resource utilization metrics (such as CPU and memory) of the Pods it targets.
2. **Metrics Gathering:** To perform auto-scaling, the HPA collects resource utilization metrics from the Pods it manages. These metrics are typically provided by the Metrics Server in the cluster, which scrapes data from various sources, including the kubelet on each node.
3. **Target Metrics and Thresholds:** You define the target resource utilization metrics and thresholds in the HPA's configuration. For example, you can set a target CPU utilization of 50%. When the average CPU utilization across all target Pods exceeds this threshold, the HPA takes action.

4. **Decision Logic:** The HPA uses the gathered metrics and thresholds to make scaling decisions. It calculates the desired number of Pods needed to maintain the target metric levels. If the current number of Pods is less than the desired number, the HPA scales up by creating new Pods. If it's more, the HPA scales down by terminating excess Pods.

5. **Scaling Action:** Once the HPA determines the scaling action (up or down), it updates the desired number of replicas in the target resource, such as a Deployment or ReplicaSet.

6. **Control Loop:** Kubernetes operates auto-scaling as a control loop, periodically checking the resource utilization metrics and making adjustments. You can specify the interval at which the HPA checks metrics in the HPA's configuration.

7. **Custom Metrics and External Metrics:** While the HPA primarily uses built-in metrics like CPU and memory, you can also configure it to use custom metrics or external metrics provided by Prometheus or other monitoring systems. This allows you to base auto-scaling decisions on application-specific metrics.

8. **Event-Driven Scaling:** In addition to resource-based scaling, Kubernetes allows you to implement event-driven scaling using custom webhooks and triggers. This enables you to respond to application-specific events or conditions outside of resource utilization metrics.

9. **Pod Lifecycle:** Pods are managed through the usual Kubernetes mechanisms. When scaling up, new Pods are created based on the Pod template defined in the target resource (e.g., Deployment). When scaling down, excess Pods are terminated, typically in a controlled and safe manner.

10. **Auto Scaling Integration:** Kubernetes integrates with cloud providers to enable **Cluster Auto Scaling**, which automatically adjusts the number of nodes in a cluster based on the resource demands of the Pods. This ensures that there are enough nodes to accommodate scaled-up Pods.

Kubernetes auto-scaling is a powerful feature for optimizing resource utilization and maintaining application performance under varying workloads. It is commonly used in conjunction with other Kubernetes components like the Horizontal Pod Autoscaler (HPA),

Metrics Server, and cloud provider integrations to automate the scaling of applications and clusters.

What are Horizontal Pod Autoscalers (HPAs) in Kubernetes?

Horizontal Pod Autoscalers (HPAs) are Kubernetes resources that allow you to automatically adjust the number of replica Pods in a Deployment, ReplicaSet, or StatefulSet based on resource utilization metrics or custom criteria. HPAs are a fundamental component for enabling auto-scaling in Kubernetes and ensuring that your applications can efficiently handle varying levels of traffic.

Here are the key characteristics and components of Horizontal Pod Autoscalers:

1. **Resource Metrics:** HPAs monitor resource utilization metrics such as CPU and memory usage of the Pods they target. These metrics are collected by the Kubernetes Metrics Server, which scrapes data from the kubelet on each node.
2. **Scaling Metrics and Thresholds:** In the HPA configuration, you define the target resource utilization metrics (e.g., CPU utilization) and the desired thresholds (e.g., 50% CPU usage). The HPA uses these metrics and thresholds to determine when to scale Pods.
3. **Desired Replica Count:** The HPA calculates the desired number of replica Pods needed to maintain the target metric levels. For example, if CPU utilization exceeds the defined threshold, the HPA may decide to scale up by increasing the replica count.
4. **Target Resource:** HPAs target specific resources in your cluster, such as a Deployment, ReplicaSet, or StatefulSet. The HPA scales the number of replica Pods associated with the target resource.
5. **Control Loop:** Auto-scaling is performed as a control loop within Kubernetes. The HPA periodically checks the resource utilization metrics and compares them to the specified thresholds.

Based on this comparison, it determines whether scaling actions are required.

6. **Scaling Actions:** When the HPA decides to scale, it can perform scaling actions like creating new Pods (scaling up) or terminating existing Pods (scaling down). Kubernetes handles these actions in a controlled and orchestrated manner.

7. **Min and Max Values:** You can configure the minimum and maximum number of replica Pods allowed for a target resource. These limits ensure that auto-scaling doesn't go beyond predefined boundaries.

8. **Custom Metrics:** While HPAs primarily use built-in metrics like CPU and memory, Kubernetes allows you to configure custom metrics or use external metrics provided by monitoring systems like Prometheus. This enables more advanced auto-scaling based on application-specific metrics.

9. **Event-Driven Scaling:** In addition to resource-based scaling, Kubernetes supports event-driven scaling through custom webhooks and triggers. This allows you to respond to application-specific events or conditions outside of resource utilization metrics.

10. **Integration with Cloud Providers:** Kubernetes can integrate with cloud providers to enable **Cluster Auto Scaling**, automatically adjusting the number of nodes in a cluster based on the resource demands of the Pods. This ensures there are enough nodes to accommodate scaled-up Pods.

Horizontal Pod Autoscalers are a powerful tool for optimizing resource utilization, ensuring high availability, and controlling costs in Kubernetes environments. They provide a straightforward way to implement auto-scaling logic, allowing your applications to adapt to changing workloads efficiently.

How does Kubernetes handle load balancing for services?

Kubernetes provides load balancing for services through a combination of features and components, ensuring that traffic is distributed evenly among the Pods that belong to a Service. Here's how Kubernetes handles load balancing for services:

1. **Service Abstraction:** Kubernetes abstracts the details of Pods and their IPs by introducing the concept of a **Service**. A Service is a stable and abstract endpoint that represents a group of Pods with a common label selector. Services provide a single entry point for accessing one or more Pods, even as Pods are created, terminated, or rescheduled.

2. **Service Types:**
   o **ClusterIP**: By default, Kubernetes creates a virtual IP address (ClusterIP) for a Service. This IP address is only reachable from within the cluster, making it suitable for internal service-to-service communication.
   o **NodePort**: NodePort Services expose the Service on a static port across all nodes in the cluster. Traffic directed to any node's IP address on the specified port is forwarded to the Service's Pods.
   o **LoadBalancer**: In cloud-based Kubernetes deployments, LoadBalancer Services leverage the cloud provider's load balancer solution to distribute external traffic across the Service's Pods. This allows for automatic provisioning of external load balancers.
   o **ExternalName**: This type maps the Service to an external DNS name. It's useful when you want to provide a DNS alias for an external service outside the cluster.

3. **Internal Load Balancing (ClusterIP):** When a Service is created with type ClusterIP, Kubernetes sets up internal load balancing. Requests to the Service's ClusterIP are distributed among the Pods behind the Service using iptables rules or IPVS (IP Virtual Server) in the Linux kernel. This ensures that each Pod in the Service receives a fair share of the traffic.

4. **NodePort Load Balancing:** NodePort Services expose the Service on a high-numbered port on each node. A kube-proxy component on each node forwards traffic from this port to one of the Pods in the Service. The Service's IP address is not used externally; instead, traffic is directed to any node's IP address and the specified port.

5. **External Load Balancing (LoadBalancer):** In cloud-based Kubernetes deployments (e.g., AWS, GCP, Azure), the LoadBalancer Service type integrates with the cloud provider's

load balancer solution. The cloud provider provisions an external load balancer that distributes external traffic to the Service's Pods. This allows for scalability and high availability of externally accessible services.

6. **Session Affinity:** By default, Services distribute traffic to Pods randomly. However, you can configure session affinity (sticky sessions) using the sessionAffinity field in the Service configuration. This ensures that client requests from the same source IP address are directed to the same Pod, which can be useful for maintaining session state.

7. **Service Discovery:** Kubernetes provides built-in DNS-based service discovery. Each Service is assigned a DNS record in the cluster's DNS system, making it easy for other Pods and Services to discover and connect to Services using their DNS names.

8. **Health Checks:** Kubernetes can perform health checks on Pods using readiness and liveness probes. These checks ensure that only healthy Pods receive traffic from Services, improving the overall reliability of load balancing.

Kubernetes handles load balancing transparently, abstracting the complexities of distributing traffic among Pods. This load balancing ensures that your applications can scale horizontally and maintain high availability as Pods are added, removed, or rescheduled within the cluster. Whether you're dealing with internal service-to-service communication or exposing services externally, Kubernetes provides the necessary mechanisms for efficient load balancing.

Explain the difference between Ingress and Service Load Balancing.

Ingress and **Service Load Balancing** are both mechanisms in Kubernetes for routing and load balancing network traffic, but they serve different purposes and operate at different layers of the network stack. Here's a breakdown of the key differences between Ingress and Service Load Balancing:

1. Layer of Operation:

- **Ingress:** Ingress operates at the application layer (Layer 7) of the OSI model. It is specifically designed for HTTP and HTTPS traffic and can perform advanced routing, path-based routing, and SSL termination.
- **Service Load Balancing:** Service Load Balancing operates at the transport layer (Layer 4) of the OSI model. It provides simple TCP/UDP-based load balancing without awareness of the content or structure of the traffic.

2. Use Cases:

- **Ingress:** Ingress is primarily used for routing external HTTP and HTTPS traffic into the cluster. It is suitable for scenarios where you need to expose multiple services through a single entry point and perform complex routing based on URL paths or hostnames.
- **Service Load Balancing:** Service Load Balancing is used for load balancing traffic between Pods within the cluster. It distributes traffic to a set of backend Pods associated with a Kubernetes Service. It's suitable for internal service-to-service communication and for exposing services that don't require advanced HTTP routing.

3. Features:

- **Ingress:** Ingress controllers can provide features like SSL termination (HTTPS), host-based routing, path-based routing, header-based routing, URL rewrites, and more. It is highly configurable and can be extended with custom annotations.
- **Service Load Balancing:** Service Load Balancing primarily provides basic TCP/UDP load balancing. It doesn't offer advanced HTTP-specific features like URL-based routing or SSL termination.

4. External vs. Internal Traffic:

- **Ingress:** Ingress is typically used to manage external traffic that originates from clients outside the Kubernetes cluster. It allows you to define rules for how external traffic should be directed to different Services within the cluster.

- **Service Load Balancing:** Service Load Balancing is used for both external and internal traffic within the cluster. It is used to distribute traffic among Pods associated with a Service, ensuring that requests are load-balanced across multiple Pods.

5. Network Layer:

- **Ingress:** Ingress controllers often utilize Kubernetes Services to route traffic to backend Pods. This means that traffic is initially directed to a Service, and the Service Load Balancing mechanism handles distribution to the Pods.
- **Service Load Balancing:** Service Load Balancing directly distributes traffic to Pods associated with a Service, bypassing the need for a separate Ingress resource.

6. Resources:

- **Ingress:** In Kubernetes, you define Ingress resources to configure routing rules for external HTTP/HTTPS traffic. Ingress resources are typically managed by an Ingress controller.
- **Service Load Balancing:** You create Kubernetes Services to define how traffic should be load-balanced among Pods. These Services are managed directly by Kubernetes and don't require an Ingress resource for internal load balancing.

9 SECURITY IN KUBERNETES

What are some best practices for securing a Kubernetes cluster?

Securing a Kubernetes cluster is crucial to protect your applications, data, and infrastructure. Here are some best practices for securing a Kubernetes cluster:

1. **Keep Kubernetes Up to Date:**
   o Regularly update Kubernetes to the latest stable version to benefit from security patches and improvements.
2. **Role-Based Access Control (RBAC):**
   o Implement RBAC to restrict access based on roles and permissions. Ensure that users and services have the least privilege required to perform their tasks.
3. **Pod Security Policies (PSPs):**
   o Use Pod Security Policies to enforce security standards for Pods. Define policies that control host namespaces, volumes, capabilities, and other security settings.
4. **Network Policies:**
   o Define Network Policies to control ingress and egress traffic between Pods. Isolate workloads and restrict communication to the necessary components.
5. **Secrets Management:**

o Store sensitive information like API tokens, database credentials, and TLS certificates in Kubernetes Secrets. Avoid storing secrets in application code or configuration files.

6. **Implement Image Security:**
   o Scan container images for vulnerabilities before deployment. Use tools like Trivy, Clair, or Anchore to identify and remediate security issues.

7. **Security Contexts:**
   o Apply security contexts to Pods and containers to set security boundaries. Configure user and group settings, and leverage SELinux or AppArmor profiles for additional protection.

8. **Use Network Encryption:**
   o Enable encryption for communication within the cluster and between clusters. Implement encryption for etcd, the Kubernetes API server, and network traffic using tools like Calico or Istio.

9. **API Server Access Control:**
   o Limit access to the Kubernetes API server by using network policies, firewalls, and client certificates. Implement API server authentication and authorization mechanisms.

10. **Audit and Monitor:**
    o Enable auditing of Kubernetes API server activities and monitor cluster components for suspicious activities. Use tools like Falco, Auditd, and the Kubernetes Audit Logging feature.

11. **Secure etcd:**
    o Protect the etcd data store, which stores cluster configuration and secrets. Implement encryption at rest, access controls, and regular backups.

12. **Limit Node Access:**
    o Restrict direct access to cluster nodes. Limit SSH access, and apply security patches and updates to nodes regularly.

13. **Implement Network Segmentation:**
    o Isolate critical components like the Kubernetes control plane from application workloads by implementing network segmentation and security groups.

14. **Regular Backups:**
    o Backup critical cluster components, including etcd, to ensure data recovery in case of failure or security incidents.

15. **Container Runtime Security:**
    o   Secure the container runtime environment (e.g., Docker) by enabling security features like seccomp and AppArmor. Use container-specific security tools like Podman and gVisor.
16. **Third-Party Security Solutions:**
    o   Explore and consider using third-party security solutions, such as runtime security scanners, network security platforms, and threat detection tools.
17. **Security Training and Awareness:**
    o   Educate your team about Kubernetes security best practices. Promote security awareness and encourage responsible handling of secrets and credentials.
18. **External Threat Detection:**
    o   Implement external threat detection and response mechanisms to identify and mitigate attacks from external sources.
19. **Compliance and Auditing:**
    o   Ensure that your Kubernetes setup complies with industry-specific regulations (e.g., GDPR, HIPAA) and perform regular security audits.
20. **Incident Response Plan:**
    o   Develop an incident response plan that outlines procedures for handling security incidents, including communication, investigation, and recovery.

Securing a Kubernetes cluster is an ongoing process that requires vigilance and adaptation to new threats and vulnerabilities. Regularly review and update your security practices to ensure the continued protection of your cluster and the applications running on it.

How does Role-Based Access Control (RBAC) work in Kubernetes?

Role-Based Access Control (RBAC) is a crucial security feature in Kubernetes that allows you to define and enforce fine-grained access policies for users, service accounts, and groups within a Kubernetes cluster. RBAC enables administrators to specify what actions (verbs) are allowed on which resources (nouns) by whom (subjects). Here's how RBAC works in Kubernetes:

1. **Subjects:**
o **Users:** Kubernetes RBAC can be used with users authenticated through various mechanisms, such as client certificates, bearer tokens, or other identity providers (e.g., OIDC).
o **Service Accounts:** Service accounts are a special type of subject used for granting permissions to workloads (Pods) running within the cluster.
o **Groups:** Users and service accounts can be organized into groups, simplifying the management of permissions for multiple entities.
2. **Resources (API Objects):**
o Kubernetes resources, often referred to as API objects, include Pods, Services, ConfigMaps, Deployments, and many others. RBAC allows you to specify which resources can be accessed and what actions can be performed on them.
3. **Verbs:**
o RBAC defines a set of verbs that represent actions that can be performed on resources. Common verbs include "get," "list," "create," "update," "delete," "patch," and "watch."
4. **Roles and ClusterRoles:**
o In Kubernetes, you define roles (for namespaced resources) and cluster roles (for cluster-wide resources). A **Role** contains rules that specify what actions are allowed on specific resources within a namespace.
o A **ClusterRole** is similar to a Role but applies to cluster-wide resources. Cluster roles can be used to grant permissions across all namespaces in a cluster.
5. **RoleBindings and ClusterRoleBindings:**
o A **RoleBinding** associates a Role (or ClusterRole) with one or more subjects (users, service accounts, or groups) within a specific namespace.
o A **ClusterRoleBinding** performs the same function as a RoleBinding but applies at the cluster level, allowing you to grant permissions across all namespaces.
6. **Evaluation Process:**

- o When a user or service account attempts to perform an action in the cluster, Kubernetes evaluates RBAC policies.
- o The system checks if the subject (user or service account) making the request matches any of the bindings (RoleBindings or ClusterRoleBindings) in the cluster.
- o If a match is found, Kubernetes checks if the requested action (verb) is allowed by the associated Role or ClusterRole.
- o If both the subject and the action are allowed by the RBAC policies, the request is granted; otherwise, it's denied.

7. **Default Roles and ClusterRoles:**
   - o Kubernetes provides a set of default roles and cluster roles that grant basic permissions for common use cases. You can use these as a starting point and customize them to suit your needs.

8. **RBAC Resources:**
   - o RBAC resources (Role, ClusterRole, RoleBinding, and ClusterRoleBinding) are defined in YAML or JSON files. You create and manage these resources using the kubectl command-line tool or by applying manifests via kubectl apply.

9. **Namespace Isolation:**
   - o RBAC policies are typically defined at the namespace level, providing isolation and control over resources within each namespace. Cluster-wide RBAC policies can also be defined for broader access control.

RBAC is a powerful mechanism for controlling access and enforcing security policies in a Kubernetes cluster. It allows administrators to tailor permissions based on the principle of least privilege, ensuring that users and service accounts have only the necessary permissions to perform their tasks, thereby enhancing the security of the cluster.

What is a Service Account, and how is it used for security?

A **Service Account** in Kubernetes is an identity associated with a Pod that is used to authenticate and authorize the actions performed by that Pod within the cluster. Service accounts are a fundamental component of Kubernetes security and play a crucial role in ensuring the principle of least privilege, where Pods and containers have only the necessary permissions to perform their tasks. Here's how Service Accounts are used for security:

1. **Authentication:**
   o When a Pod is created, it can be associated with a specific Service Account. This association is established via the serviceAccountName field in the Pod's configuration.
   o Kubernetes uses Service Accounts to authenticate the identity of Pods and their associated containers when they interact with the Kubernetes API server and other cluster resources.
2. **Authorization:**
   o Once the identity of a Pod is established through the Service Account, Kubernetes RBAC (Role-Based Access Control) mechanisms can be used to determine what actions the Pod is authorized to perform within the cluster.
   o RBAC policies can be configured to grant specific permissions to Service Accounts, allowing fine-grained control over what resources and actions Pods associated with a particular Service Account can access.
3. **Least Privilege Principle:**
   o Service Accounts are a critical tool for implementing the principle of least privilege. By associating each Pod with a specific Service Account and configuring RBAC policies accordingly, you ensure that Pods have only the necessary permissions for their intended tasks.
   o This limits the potential impact of security breaches or vulnerabilities in Pods, as attackers can only exploit the permissions granted to the associated Service Account.
4. **Secrets Management:**
   o Service Accounts automatically have associated secrets (Kubernetes API tokens) stored in the cluster. These tokens are mounted into Pods at a specific path (e.g., /var/run/secrets/kubernetes.io/serviceaccount/token), allowing Pods to authenticate with the Kubernetes API server.
   o Service Account tokens can also be used to securely access other resources within the cluster, such as Kubernetes Secrets and ConfigMaps, by setting appropriate RBAC policies.

5. **Namespace Scope:**
   o Service Accounts are typically scoped to a specific namespace. This means that they are only available and applicable within that namespace.
   o By isolating Service Accounts to namespaces, you can enforce a security boundary that prevents Pods in one namespace from interfering with or accessing resources in other namespaces.
6. **Cluster-Wide Service Accounts:**
   o While most Service Accounts are scoped to individual namespaces, Kubernetes also supports cluster-wide Service Accounts (ServiceAccount resources defined in the kube-system namespace, for example). These are used for managing cluster-level resources and components.
7. **Default Service Account:**
   o Every namespace has a default Service Account automatically created. If you don't specify a Service Account for a Pod, it uses the default Service Account of the namespace. Be cautious when using the default Service Account, as it may have more permissions than necessary.

How can you scan container images for vulnerabilities in Kubernetes?

Scanning container images for vulnerabilities in Kubernetes is a crucial part of securing your containerized applications. Vulnerability scanning helps identify and remediate security issues in the software packages and libraries bundled in your container images. Here's how you can scan container images for vulnerabilities in Kubernetes:

1. **Container Image Scanning Tools:**
   o There are several container image scanning tools and services available, both open-source and commercial. Some popular options include:
   ▪ **Trivy:** An open-source vulnerability scanner for containers and other artifacts. Trivy supports scanning Docker images, as well as images in containerd, OCI, and more.

- **Clair:** An open-source vulnerability scanner that focuses on analyzing layers in container images. Clair is commonly used with tools like **Quay** or **Clairctl** for vulnerability assessment.
- **Anchore:** A container image inspection and analysis tool that checks for known vulnerabilities, software configurations, and compliance issues.
- **Sysdig Secure:** A commercial container security platform that includes image scanning capabilities.
- **Aqua Security:** A commercial platform offering container image scanning and runtime security features.
  - Choose a scanning tool that aligns with your specific needs and integrates well with your CI/CD pipeline and Kubernetes cluster.

2. **Integrate Scanning into the CI/CD Pipeline:**
   - Implement image scanning as part of your CI/CD (Continuous Integration/Continuous Deployment) pipeline. Most scanning tools provide plugins or integrations for popular CI/CD platforms like Jenkins, GitLab CI/CD, and CircleCI.
   - Configure the scanning step to run automatically when building or pushing container images to your image registry.

3. **Image Registry Integration:**
   - Integrate vulnerability scanning with your container image registry. Some container registries offer built-in scanning or support for third-party scanning tools.
   - For example, **Docker Hub** and **GitHub Container Registry** offer integrated image scanning capabilities.

4. **Scheduled Scans:**
   - Set up regular, scheduled scans for your container images, especially for images in production use. Vulnerabilities can emerge over time, so continuous monitoring is essential.

5. **Scan on Image Update:**
   - Trigger vulnerability scans whenever a new image is pushed to the registry or an existing image is updated. This ensures that you are aware of vulnerabilities in the latest image versions.

6. **Vulnerability Database Updates:**

o Keep the vulnerability database used by your scanning tool up to date. Vulnerability databases are regularly updated to include new security vulnerabilities and their severity ratings.

7. **Severity Thresholds:**
   o Define severity thresholds for vulnerabilities based on your organization's risk tolerance. High-severity vulnerabilities may require immediate action, while low-severity ones can be addressed in a more planned manner.

8. **Scan Results Integration:**
   o Integrate the scan results with your Kubernetes cluster or security information and event management (SIEM) system. This allows you to centralize and monitor vulnerabilities and take appropriate actions.

9. **Automated Remediation:**
   o Consider implementing automated remediation steps as part of your CI/CD pipeline. For example, you can automatically rebuild and redeploy containers with updated base images or patched dependencies.

10. **Manual Review and Mitigation:**
    o Review scan results and take appropriate manual actions to address vulnerabilities that cannot be remediated automatically. This may involve modifying your application code or configurations.

11. **Documentation and Policy:**
    o Establish clear policies and procedures for addressing vulnerabilities. Document how vulnerabilities are identified, assessed, and mitigated to ensure consistency across your organization.

12. **Regular Audit and Review:**
    o Periodically review your scanning process and results to improve your security practices. Ensure that you are addressing vulnerabilities promptly and effectively.

By implementing container image scanning as an integral part of your Kubernetes workflow, you can proactively identify and mitigate vulnerabilities, reducing the risk of security breaches and ensuring the overall security of your containerized applications.

10 UPGRADES AND ROLLBACKS

What is the process for upgrading a Kubernetes cluster?

Upgrading a Kubernetes cluster is a critical maintenance task to ensure that your cluster benefits from the latest features, security patches, and bug fixes. The process involves upgrading the control plane components, worker nodes, and any add-ons or plugins. Here's a general process for upgrading a Kubernetes cluster:

1. Backup Your Cluster:

- Before starting the upgrade process, ensure that you have reliable backups of your cluster's configuration, etcd data, and any critical applications or data. This is a crucial step to ensure you can recover in case of issues during the upgrade.

2. Review Release Notes:

- Check the release notes for the new version of Kubernetes you plan to upgrade to. Pay attention to any breaking changes, deprecated features, or known issues that might affect your cluster.

3. Plan the Upgrade:

- Develop a comprehensive upgrade plan that includes the following:
  - A schedule for the upgrade, considering the impact on your applications and users.
  - A rollback plan in case the upgrade encounters issues.
  - Testing procedures for validating the upgrade in a staging environment.
  - Communication with stakeholders to inform them of the upgrade timeline.

4. Upgrade etcd:

- If your cluster uses a separate etcd cluster (common in production deployments), upgrade etcd to a version compatible with the new Kubernetes version. Ensure you follow etcd's upgrade process and backup etcd data.

5. Upgrade Control Plane Components:

- Upgrade the control plane components, including the Kubernetes API server, controller manager, scheduler, and any other components running on the master nodes.
- This can typically be done one component at a time. Follow the documentation specific to your Kubernetes distribution or installation method for detailed instructions on upgrading these components.

6. Upgrade Worker Nodes:

- Upgrade the worker nodes (also known as worker or minion nodes) in your cluster. This involves upgrading the kubelet and kube-proxy components on each node.
- You can usually perform rolling upgrades, meaning you upgrade one node at a time, allowing your applications to continue running with minimal disruption.

7. Upgrade Add-ons and Plugins:

- If your cluster uses any add-ons or plugins, such as network plugins (e.g., Calico, Flannel), monitoring tools (e.g., Prometheus, Grafana), or log aggregators (e.g., Elasticsearch, Fluentd), ensure that these are compatible with the new Kubernetes version and upgrade them as needed.

8. Verify and Test:

- After upgrading control plane components, worker nodes, and add-ons, thoroughly test your cluster to ensure that applications are running as expected and that there are no issues or regressions.
- Use a staging environment to validate the upgrade before applying it to your production cluster.

9. Monitor and Rollback (if Necessary):

- Monitor your cluster closely during and after the upgrade to detect any anomalies or performance issues. Be prepared to rollback to the previous version if critical problems arise.
- If a rollback is necessary, follow your rollback plan and verify that the cluster is functioning correctly in the previous state.

10. Update API Objects and Resources: - Some Kubernetes API objects may need updates to work with the new version. For example, custom resource definitions (CRDs) may require updates. - Update any deprecated or obsolete API objects according to the new version's specifications.

11. Communicate and Document: - Keep stakeholders informed about the upgrade progress and its impact. Document the upgrade process, including any changes or configurations made during the upgrade.

12. Post-Upgrade Tasks: - After successful completion of the upgrade, perform any post-upgrade tasks, such as optimizing configurations, reviewing security settings, and ensuring compliance with your organization's policies.

Remember that the specific steps and procedures for upgrading a Kubernetes cluster may vary depending on your deployment method (e.g., managed Kubernetes service, self-hosted), the Kubernetes distribution you use, and any custom configurations in your cluster. Always consult the official documentation and guidelines provided by your Kubernetes distribution or platform for detailed instructions on upgrading your specific setup.

How can you roll back to a previous version of an application in Kubernetes?

Rolling back to a previous version of an application in Kubernetes involves reverting your application to a prior deployment state. Kubernetes provides mechanisms for managing these rollbacks effectively. Here's a step-by-step guide on how to roll back an application to a previous version:

1. Identify the Previous Version:

- Determine the specific version or revision of your application that you want to roll back to. This could be a previous deployment, replica set, or image version.

2. Inspect Deployment History:

- Use the kubectl rollout history command to view the deployment history of your application. This command will display a list of revisions with their respective details, such as the revision number and any annotations.

```
kubectl rollout history deployment/<deployment-name>
```

3. Choose the Revision to Roll Back To:

- Select the revision number corresponding to the version you want to roll back to. Note that revisions are numbered sequentially.

4. Roll Back the Deployment:

- Use the kubectl rollout undo command to initiate the rollback to the chosen revision. Specify the deployment name and the revision number.

```
kubectl rollout undo deployment/<deployment-name> --to-revision=<revision-number>
```

Replace <deployment-name> with the name of your deployment and <revision-number> with the chosen revision number.

5. Monitor the Rollback:

- Use kubectl get pods and other relevant commands to monitor the status of the rollback. Pods from the new version may be terminated, and pods from the previous version will be created.

```
kubectl get pods
```

6. Validate the Rollback:

- Test your application to ensure that it has successfully rolled back to the previous version. Check for any issues or regressions to confirm that the rollback was successful.

7. Optional: Lock the Deployment:

- To prevent accidental changes to the deployment, consider applying a deployment lock using labels or annotations. This can help prevent automatic scaling or further rollouts until the lock is removed.

8. Document the Rollback:

- Update your documentation and incident reports to include details of the rollback, including the revision number and any issues that triggered the rollback.

9. Continuous Improvement:

- After rolling back, investigate the root cause of the issue that prompted the rollback. Implement necessary fixes and improvements to prevent similar issues in the future.

10. Remove Lock (if applied): - If you applied a deployment lock, make sure to remove it when you're confident that the rollback was successful and the issues have been resolved.

Rolling back to a previous version in Kubernetes is a valuable feature for managing and maintaining your applications, especially in the face of unexpected issues or regressions. It allows you to quickly restore a known, stable state while providing the opportunity to diagnose and address problems without significant downtime.

Explain the concept of "rolling updates" in Kubernetes.

In Kubernetes, **rolling updates** refer to a deployment strategy used to update applications to a new version or configuration while minimizing downtime and ensuring that the transition is as smooth as possible. Rolling updates gradually replace old instances of an application with new ones, ensuring that there is no point in time when the entire application is offline. This strategy is particularly important for maintaining the availability and reliability of applications in production environments.

Here's how rolling updates work in Kubernetes:

1. **Replica Sets:**
o Rolling updates are often managed through the use of **Replica Sets** or, more commonly, **Deployments**. A Deployment is a higher-level resource that manages Replica Sets and ensures that a specified number of Pods are running and available.
2. **Specifying the Desired State:**

o   When you create or update a Deployment resource, you specify the desired state of your application, including the container image, the number of replicas (Pods), and any configuration changes.

3. **Gradual Replacement:**
   o   Kubernetes orchestrates the update by gradually replacing the old Pods (instances of the application) with new ones that adhere to the desired state. It does this in a controlled manner, typically one Pod at a time.

4. **Health Checks:**
   o   Kubernetes continuously monitors the health of both old and new Pods during the update process. Health checks (readiness and liveness probes) are used to ensure that new Pods are ready to serve traffic before old Pods are terminated.

5. **Scaling:**
   o   If scaling is part of the update strategy (e.g., increasing the number of replicas), Kubernetes adjusts the number of Pods accordingly. This can involve scaling up or down as needed.

6. **Rollback Mechanism:**
   o   If an issue is detected during the rolling update, Kubernetes provides a rollback mechanism. You can easily revert to the previous version of your application by using the kubectl rollout undo command.

7. **Customization and Configuration:**
   o   Rolling updates can be customized to suit your application's requirements. You can specify parameters like the maximum surge (number of additional Pods to create at once), the maximum unavailable (number of Pods that can be taken offline at once), and more.

8. **Monitoring and Observability:**
   o   During a rolling update, you can monitor the status and progress using commands like kubectl get pods and check events and logs for any issues.

9. **Completion and Verification:**
   o   Once all the old Pods have been replaced with new ones, the rolling update is considered complete. You can verify the application's behavior and performance to ensure that it meets expectations.

Rolling updates are a fundamental part of managing applications in Kubernetes, providing a balance between continuous delivery of updates and maintaining the desired level of service availability. They are particularly useful for applications that require high availability and cannot afford significant downtime during updates or configuration changes.

11 TROUBLESHOOTING AND DEBUGGING

What are common issues that arise in Kubernetes, and how do you troubleshoot them?

In Kubernetes, like any complex system, a variety of issues can arise that impact the availability, performance, and reliability of your applications. Troubleshooting these issues is a crucial skill for Kubernetes administrators and developers. Here are some common issues that you might encounter in Kubernetes, along with troubleshooting steps:

1. Pod Scheduling Issues:

- **Issue:** Pods are not getting scheduled to nodes.
- **Troubleshooting:**
  - Check the resource requests and limits defined in your Pod specs.
  - Ensure that your nodes have enough available resources (CPU, memory) to accommodate the Pods.
  - Investigate node taints and tolerations or node affinity/anti-affinity rules.

- o Examine Pod affinity and anti-affinity rules if they are preventing placement.
- o Review the output of kubectl describe pod <pod-name> for scheduling-related events and errors.

2. Application Crashes:

- **Issue:** Pods or containers within Pods are crashing or failing to start.
- **Troubleshooting:**
  - o Check container logs for error messages using kubectl logs.
  - o Inspect Pod events with kubectl describe pod <pod-name> to identify issues.
  - o Verify that the container image and its entrypoint/command are correctly configured.
  - o Ensure that required environment variables and configuration files are correctly provided.
- o Review resource requests and limits to prevent resource exhaustion.

3. Networking Problems:

- **Issue:** Pods cannot communicate with each other or external services.
- **Troubleshooting:**
  - o Confirm that your network plugin (e.g., Calico, Flannel) is properly installed and running.
  - o Check Pod IP addresses using kubectl get pods -o wide and verify that they are in the expected range.
  - o Review Network Policies to ensure that they are not blocking traffic.
  - o Check for Pod, Service, and Ingress misconfigurations.
- o Examine DNS resolution within the cluster (nslookup, dig).

4. Resource Constraints:

- **Issue:** Pods or applications are experiencing resource contention.
- **Troubleshooting:**

o Monitor resource usage using tools like Prometheus, Grafana, or Kubernetes Dashboard.
o Check resource requests and limits in Pod specifications and adjust them as needed.
o Use Horizontal Pod Autoscalers (HPAs) to automatically scale Pods based on resource utilization.

5. Control Plane Issues:

- **Issue:** Control plane components (API server, etcd, controller manager, scheduler) are experiencing problems.
- **Troubleshooting:**
  o Check the health and logs of control plane components using kubectl get componentstatuses and kubectl logs.
  o Investigate the cluster's etcd health and perform backups and maintenance.
o Ensure there are no resource constraints on control plane nodes.

6. Node Failures:

- **Issue:** Nodes become unresponsive or are frequently restarting.
- **Troubleshooting:**
  o Inspect node status and conditions using kubectl get nodes and kubectl describe node <node-name>.
  o Check system logs (journalctl or dmesg) on the affected node for hardware or kernel issues.
  o Investigate the kubelet logs on the node.
o Use node management tools like Kubernetes Node Problem Detector to identify hardware issues.

7. Storage Problems:

- **Issue:** Persistent Volumes (PVs) or Persistent Volume Claims (PVCs) are not working as expected.
- **Troubleshooting:**
  o Examine the status of PVs and PVCs with kubectl get pv and kubectl get pvc.
  o Check if the storage provider (e.g., AWS EBS, GCP PD) has any issues.

o   Verify that the storage classes are correctly configured.
o   Review access modes and reclaim policies of PVs.

8. Security Incidents:

- **Issue:** Security breaches or vulnerabilities are detected.
- **Troubleshooting:**
    o   Investigate the extent of the security incident.
    o   Analyze logs, audit trails, and network traffic for signs of unauthorized access.
    o   Follow incident response procedures to mitigate and recover from the incident.
    o   Apply security patches and implement measures to prevent future incidents.

9. Configuration Errors:

- **Issue:** Configuration files, secrets, or environment variables are incorrect.
- **Troubleshooting:**
    o   Review the configuration of your application and check for errors.
    o   Inspect ConfigMaps, Secrets, and environment variables.
    o   Validate the correctness of configuration files and mounted volumes.
    o   Use tools like kubectl describe to gather information about resource configurations.

In addition to the steps mentioned for each issue, Kubernetes provides extensive debugging and troubleshooting tools such as kubectl, container runtime logs, kubectl describe, and monitoring and observability solutions like Prometheus and Grafana. A well-documented and rehearsed incident response plan is also crucial for addressing unexpected issues promptly and effectively.

How can you access the logs of a running Pod?

To access the logs of a running Pod in Kubernetes, you can use the kubectl logs command. Here's how you can do it:

1. **Basic Log Retrieval:**

   To view the logs of a running Pod, use the `kubectl logs` command followed by the name of the Pod:

```
kubectl logs <pod-name>
```

Replace <pod-name> with the actual name of the Pod you want to access the logs for.

- **Specify a Container:**

If a Pod has multiple containers, you can specify which container's logs you want to view by using the -c or --container flag:

```
kubectl logs <pod-name> -c <container-name>
```

Replace <container-name> with the name of the container whose logs you want to retrieve.

- **Timestamps and Previous Containers:**

To include timestamps in the log output and view logs from previous containers (if a container has restarted), you can use the -t or --timestamps and -p or --previous flags, respectively:

```
kubectl logs -t -p <pod-name> -c <container-name>
```

- **Tail the Logs:**

By default, kubectl logs provides the most recent log entries. You can specify the number of lines to show from the end of the log using the -n or --tail flag:

```
kubectl logs --tail=50 <pod-name>
```

This command would show the last 50 lines of logs.

- **Stream Logs in Real-Time:**

To stream the logs in real-time (similar to tail -f), you can use the -f or --follow flag:

```
kubectl logs -f <pod-name>
```

This command will continue to display new log entries as they are generated.

- **Logs from Previous Pods:**

If you have deleted a Pod but want to access its logs, you can use the --previous flag:

```
kubectl logs --previous <pod-name>
```

This command retrieves logs from the most recent terminated instance of the specified Pod.

- **Access Logs from a Specific Container in a Multi-Container Pod:**

In Pods with multiple containers, you can access logs from a specific container using the -c flag:

```
kubectl logs <pod-name> -c <container-name>
```

This command is particularly useful when troubleshooting issues in a multi-container setup.

- **Redirect Logs to a File:**

If you want to save the logs to a file, you can use shell redirection to write the logs to a file:

```
kubectl logs <pod-name> > mypodlogs.txt
```

This command saves the logs to a file named mypodlogs.txt.

By using these commands and options, you can effectively access and analyze the logs of a running Pod in Kubernetes, which is essential for debugging and monitoring the behavior of your applications.

What are some debugging tools and techniques for Kubernetes?

Debugging in Kubernetes can be complex due to the distributed and dynamic nature of containerized applications. Fortunately, there are various debugging tools and techniques available to help diagnose and resolve issues effectively. Here are some of them:

1. kubectl:

- **Describe Pods and Resources:** Use kubectl describe to get detailed information about Pods, Services, Deployments, and other resources. This can reveal important events and configurations.

```
kubectl describe pod <pod-name>
```

- **Log Retrieval:** As mentioned earlier, kubectl logs is invaluable for accessing container logs.

```
kubectl logs <pod-name>
```

- **Exec into Containers:** The kubectl exec command allows you to execute commands within a container, which is useful for debugging and running diagnostic commands.

```
kubectl exec -it <pod-name> -- /bin/sh
```

2. Monitoring and Observability Tools:

- **Prometheus and Grafana:** These open-source monitoring and alerting tools are widely used in the Kubernetes ecosystem. They can help you collect and visualize metrics, create alerts, and identify performance bottlenecks.

- **Kube-state-metrics:** This tool provides a wealth of cluster-level metrics about your Kubernetes objects. It's helpful for understanding the state of your resources.
- **cAdvisor:** The Container Advisor provides detailed container-level metrics, which can be useful for diagnosing resource-related issues.

3. Distributed Tracing:

- **Jaeger and Zipkin:** Distributed tracing tools help trace requests as they traverse through microservices. This can be essential for pinpointing performance issues in complex applications.

4. Logging and Log Aggregation:

- **Fluentd, Logstash, and Elasticsearch (ELK Stack):** These tools are used for collecting, processing, and storing logs. ELK Stack, in particular, is popular for log aggregation and visualization.
- **Loki and Grafana:** Loki is an efficient log aggregator that can be used alongside Grafana for log analysis and visualization.

5. Networking Tools:

- kubectl port-forward: This command allows you to forward a local port to a port on a running Pod. It's useful for debugging network issues by accessing services running in Pods directly.

```
kubectl port-forward <pod-name> <local-port>:<pod-port>
```

- **Wireshark and tcpdump:** For lower-level network troubleshooting, these packet capture tools can be used to inspect network traffic between Pods.

6. Kubernetes Dashboard:

- The Kubernetes Dashboard provides a web-based user interface for cluster management. It offers insights into resource utilization, Pod statuses, and other cluster-related information.

7. kubectl Debugging Plugins:

- There are several third-party kubectl plugins that extend its capabilities for debugging purposes. For example:
  o kubetail allows you to tail logs from multiple Pods at once.
  o kubens and kubectx help switch between Kubernetes namespaces and contexts, making it easier to focus on specific parts of your cluster.

8. Pod-to-Pod Communication Tools:

- curl and wget: These command-line tools can be useful for testing HTTP and network connectivity between Pods.

9. Custom Scripting:

- Sometimes, a custom script tailored to your application's specific debugging needs can be the most efficient tool. You can include diagnostic commands and logic specific to your application.

10. Chaos Engineering Tools:

```
- Tools like Chaos Mesh and LitmusChaos allow you to
perform controlled experiments to test your
application's resilience in the face of failures.
```

When debugging in Kubernetes, it's essential to follow best practices, like:

- Starting with the simplest debugging techniques and tools.
- Collecting metrics and logs proactively to identify issues before they impact production.
- Ensuring that your application is designed with observability in mind, with well-defined metrics and trace points.
- Regularly testing your troubleshooting procedures in a controlled environment.

Ultimately, the choice of tools and techniques will depend on the specific issue you're facing, the nature of your applications, and your monitoring and debugging requirements. A combination of these tools and a proactive debugging mindset will help you effectively troubleshoot and resolve issues in Kubernetes environments.

12 KUBERNETES ECOSYSTEM

What are some popular tools and projects in the Kubernetes ecosystem?

The Kubernetes ecosystem is a dynamic and ever-expanding landscape, with a multitude of tools and projects that enhance and extend Kubernetes' capabilities. Here are some popular tools and projects in the Kubernetes ecosystem, categorized by their primary use cases:

Package Management and Application Deployment:

1. **Helm:** Helm is the most widely used package manager for Kubernetes. It allows you to define, install, and upgrade even the most complex Kubernetes applications using charts.
2. **Kustomize:** Kustomize is a tool for customizing Kubernetes configurations. It enables you to manage Kubernetes resources in a more declarative and composable way.

Service Mesh and Networking:

3. **Istio:** Istio is a powerful service mesh that provides traffic management, security, and observability features for microservices running on Kubernetes.

4. **Linkerd:** Linkerd is a lightweight service mesh designed for ease of use and performance. It offers features like automatic mTLS encryption and observability.

Serverless and Event-Driven Computing:

5. **Knative:** Knative is an open-source serverless framework for Kubernetes. It simplifies the deployment of serverless applications and provides autoscaling and event-driven capabilities.
6. **OpenFaaS:** OpenFaaS is a serverless platform built on Kubernetes, allowing you to run and scale serverless functions with ease.
7. **KEDA (Kubernetes-based Event-Driven Autoscaling):** KEDA is a tool that enables event-driven autoscaling for Kubernetes Pods. It's often used in conjunction with other serverless frameworks.

Continuous Integration and Continuous Deployment (CI/CD):

8. **Jenkins X:** Jenkins X is an open-source CI/CD platform that streamlines the development and deployment of cloud-native applications on Kubernetes.
9. **ArgoCD:** ArgoCD is a declarative, GitOps continuous delivery tool for Kubernetes. It helps automate the deployment and management of applications.
10. **Tekton:** Tekton is a Kubernetes-native framework for building and deploying CI/CD pipelines. It enables the creation of custom pipelines as code.

Monitoring and Observability:

11. **Prometheus:** Prometheus is an open-source monitoring and alerting toolkit that collects and stores metrics and provides powerful querying capabilities.
12. **Grafana:** Grafana is a popular open-source platform for creating interactive dashboards and visualizing metrics from Prometheus and other data sources.

Logging and Tracing:

13. **Fluentd:** Fluentd is an open-source data collector that can collect, process, and forward logs. It's commonly used for log aggregation in Kubernetes.
14. **Elasticsearch and Kibana (ELK Stack):** Elasticsearch and Kibana are often used together with Fluentd for log storage, search, and visualization.
15. **Jaeger:** Jaeger is an open-source, end-to-end distributed tracing system for monitoring and troubleshooting microservices-based applications.

Storage Solutions:

16. **Rook:** Rook is a cloud-native storage orchestrator that brings storage services like Ceph and others to Kubernetes, enabling dynamic storage provisioning.
17. **Longhorn:** Longhorn is a cloud-native distributed storage solution for Kubernetes that provides block storage capabilities with simplicity and resilience.

Security and Compliance:

18. **Kyverno:** Kyverno is a Kubernetes-native policy engine that helps enforce policies and security controls on resource configurations.
19. **Falco:** Falco is an open-source security tool that provides runtime security monitoring and alerting for Kubernetes.

Multicloud and Hybrid Cloud Management:

20. **Crossplane:** Crossplane is an open-source multicloud control plane that helps manage cloud resources and infrastructure as code from Kubernetes.

Container Image Building and Registry:

21. **BuildKit:** BuildKit is an advanced container image builder that offers features like build caching, advanced build options, and efficient layer handling.
22. **Harbor:** Harbor is an open-source container image registry and artifact repository with security and vulnerability scanning features.

These are just a few examples of the many tools and projects available in the Kubernetes ecosystem. The choice of tools depends on your specific use case and requirements, but exploring these projects can help you leverage Kubernetes to its full potential for building and managing cloud-native applications.

How does Kubernetes integrate with container registries like Docker Hub?

Kubernetes integrates with container registries like Docker Hub to pull container images and deploy applications. Container registries serve as repositories for container images, and Kubernetes uses these images to create Pods and run containers. Here's how Kubernetes interacts with container registries:

1. **Image Definition in Kubernetes Manifests:**

    In Kubernetes manifests (such as Deployment or Pod specifications), you specify the container image to use for each container within a Pod. This image is identified by its full name, which typically includes the registry's URL, the image name, and the version (tag).

    Example:

```
spec:
  containers:
  - name: my-app
    image: docker.io/username/my-app:1.0
```

In this example, docker.io is the Docker Hub registry, username is the Docker Hub username or organization, my-app is the image name, and 1.0 is the image tag.

- **Image Pull Policy:**

Kubernetes allows you to specify an image pull policy for each container. The pull policy can be one of the following:

- Always: Kubernetes will always attempt to pull the latest image from the registry, even if a local copy exists.
- IfNotPresent: Kubernetes will use the local image if it exists; otherwise, it will attempt to pull the image.
- Never: Kubernetes will use the local image if it exists; otherwise, it will not attempt to pull the image.

The default pull policy is Always.

- **Authentication:**

To access private container registries like Docker Hub, Kubernetes needs authentication credentials. These credentials are typically stored in Kubernetes as **Secrets**. You create a Secret that contains the registry's username and password or an authentication token.

Example of creating a Secret with Docker Hub credentials:

```
kubectl create secret docker-registry my-
dockerhub-secret \
  --docker-server=docker.io \
  --docker-username=your-username \
  --docker-password=your-password \
  --docker-email=your-email
```

3. Then, you can reference this Secret in your Pod or Deployment manifest to enable authentication.
4. **Image Pulling Process:**

When you create a Pod or a Deployment that specifies an image from a container registry, Kubernetes follows this process to pull the image:

- o   It checks if the image is available locally on the node where the Pod is scheduled. If it's not present or if the pull policy is set to Always or IfNotPresent, Kubernetes proceeds to the next step.
- o   It checks for any authentication credentials (such as Secrets) associated with the registry. If credentials are available, Kubernetes uses them to authenticate with the registry.
- o   It contacts the container registry (e.g., Docker Hub) using the provided credentials and pulls the specified image.
- o   Once the image is downloaded, Kubernetes runs the container using that image.

5. **Image Updates:**

Kubernetes continuously monitors the Pods running in a cluster. If a new image version is available in the registry and a Deployment's strategy allows rolling updates, Kubernetes can automatically trigger the deployment of updated Pods.

By integrating with container registries like Docker Hub, Kubernetes simplifies the process of managing container images, ensuring that your applications always run with the latest, secure, and up-to-date images. This integration is a fundamental aspect of Kubernetes' ability to efficiently manage containerized workloads in a production environment.

13 INTERVIEW TIPS AND BEST PRACTICES

Tips for preparing for a Kubernetes interview

Preparing for a Kubernetes interview requires a combination of technical knowledge, hands-on experience, and effective communication skills. Whether you're interviewing for a Kubernetes administrator, developer, or DevOps role, here are some tips to help you prepare effectively:

1. **Understand the Basics:**
   o Start with a strong foundation by thoroughly understanding Kubernetes fundamentals, including its architecture, key components (such as Pods, Services, and Deployments), and how it manages containerized applications.
2. **Hands-On Experience:**
   o Practice deploying, managing, and troubleshooting Kubernetes clusters. Create your own clusters using tools like Minikube or kind, or use cloud-based Kubernetes services.
   o Experiment with deploying sample applications, scaling them, and managing their lifecycle.
3. **Review Documentation:**

o   Familiarize yourself with the official Kubernetes documentation. It's a valuable resource for in-depth information about Kubernetes features, configurations, and best practices.

4. **Explore Kubernetes Ecosystem:**
     o   Gain knowledge of tools and projects within the Kubernetes ecosystem, such as Helm for package management, Istio for service mesh, and Prometheus for monitoring.
     o   Understand how these tools integrate with Kubernetes and their use cases.

5. **Practice Troubleshooting:**
     o   Kubernetes interviews often include troubleshooting scenarios. Practice identifying and resolving common issues, such as Pod scheduling problems, network connectivity issues, or configuration errors.
     o   Use kubectl commands to inspect Pods, Nodes, Services, and other resources to diagnose problems.

6. **Study Common Use Cases:**
     o   Learn how Kubernetes is used in real-world scenarios. Understand how it helps with application scaling, rolling updates, and zero-downtime deployments.

7. **Master Kubernetes Networking:**
     o   Understand Kubernetes networking concepts, including Service discovery, Ingress controllers, and Network Policies.
     o   Learn about different networking plugins and how they work in various Kubernetes environments.

8. **Hands-On Kubernetes Security:**
     o   Explore Kubernetes security best practices, including Role-Based Access Control (RBAC), Pod Security Policies, and container image security.
     o   Practice securing your cluster and applications by implementing these security measures.

9. **Mock Interviews:**
     o   Conduct mock interviews with a peer or mentor to simulate the interview experience. Focus on answering technical questions effectively and explaining your thought process clearly.

10. **Behavioral Questions:**
    o Prepare responses to common behavioral questions. Use the STAR (Situation, Task, Action, Result) method to structure your answers when discussing past experiences and problem-solving abilities.

11. **Whiteboard Challenges:**
    o Practice whiteboard coding challenges. While Kubernetes interviews may not always include coding, some technical assessments involve whiteboard exercises related to Kubernetes concepts.

12. **Stay Updated:**
    o Stay current with the latest Kubernetes releases, features, and best practices. Kubernetes evolves rapidly, and interviewers may ask about recent updates.

13. **Documentation and Note-Taking:**
    o During your preparation, maintain detailed notes and create a Kubernetes cheat sheet with commonly used commands, resource definitions, and configuration examples.

14. **Ask Questions:**
    o Be prepared to ask thoughtful questions about the company's use of Kubernetes, their infrastructure, and their specific challenges. This demonstrates your interest and engagement in the role.

15. **Interview Etiquette:**
    o Dress professionally for video interviews and arrive on time (virtually) for in-person interviews.
    o Be polite, attentive, and focused during the interview.

16. **Follow-Up:**
    o Send a thank-you email after the interview to express your appreciation for the opportunity and reiterate your interest in the role.

17. **Continuous Learning:**
    o The Kubernetes landscape is dynamic. Continue to learn and stay updated even after your interview to stay competitive in the job market.

Remember that interviewers may assess not only your technical skills but also your problem-solving abilities, adaptability, and cultural fit with the organization. Therefore, it's essential to approach the interview process holistically and showcase both your technical expertise and soft skills.

Some real-world scenarios or projects to showcase your Kubernetes expertise

Showcasing your Kubernetes expertise in real-world scenarios or projects is an excellent way to demonstrate your skills to potential employers. Here are some real-world scenarios and project ideas that you can use to showcase your Kubernetes knowledge:

1. **Deploying Microservices Applications:**
   o Create a microservices-based application (e.g., e-commerce platform, social media application) and deploy it on a Kubernetes cluster. Use Kubernetes Services, Deployments, and Ingress controllers to manage and scale the microservices.
2. **CI/CD Pipelines with Kubernetes:**
   o Set up a CI/CD pipeline for a sample application using tools like Jenkins, GitLab CI/CD, or Tekton. Automate building Docker images, pushing them to a container registry, and deploying them to a Kubernetes cluster.
3. **Highly Available Cluster:**
   o Build and configure a highly available Kubernetes cluster using multiple control plane nodes and worker nodes. Implement failover and disaster recovery strategies.
4. **Kubernetes Monitoring and Alerting:**
   o Implement a comprehensive monitoring and alerting solution for your Kubernetes cluster. Use Prometheus for metrics collection, Grafana for visualization, and create alerts for critical events.
5. **Multi-Cluster Deployment:**
   o Set up multiple Kubernetes clusters (on different cloud providers or on-premises) and demonstrate how to deploy and manage applications across these clusters using federation or multi-cluster management tools.
6. **Container Orchestration for Legacy Applications:**

o Migrate a monolithic or legacy application to a containerized environment on Kubernetes. Showcase the benefits of containerization, scalability, and resource optimization.

7. **Kubernetes Security Implementation:**
   o Focus on Kubernetes security best practices. Implement RBAC policies, Pod Security Policies (PSPs), and network policies to secure your cluster. Set up security scanning for container images.

8. **Scaling and Load Balancing:**
   o Create an application that automatically scales based on metrics like CPU and memory usage. Implement Horizontal Pod Autoscalers (HPAs) and demonstrate how the application handles traffic spikes.

9. **Blue-Green Deployments:**
   o Implement a blue-green deployment strategy for an application on Kubernetes. Show how it allows for seamless updates and rollbacks with minimal downtime.

10. **GitOps Workflow:**
   o Set up a GitOps workflow using tools like ArgoCD or Flux. Manage the entire Kubernetes configuration in a Git repository, and demonstrate how changes automatically apply to the cluster.

11. **Serverless Workloads:**
   o Develop and deploy serverless functions using Knative or OpenFaaS. Showcase how Kubernetes can be used for serverless computing and event-driven architectures.

12. **Stateful Applications:**
   o Deploy stateful applications using StatefulSets. Show how to manage databases, message queues, and other stateful workloads on Kubernetes.

13. **Disaster Recovery Plan:**
   o Develop a disaster recovery plan for your Kubernetes cluster. Test backup and restore procedures for both data and configurations.

14. **Hybrid Cloud and Multicloud Deployments:**
   o Set up Kubernetes clusters in different cloud providers and demonstrate workload portability and management across them.

15. **Kubernetes Operators:**

o   Create custom Kubernetes Operators using the Operator Framework. Automate complex application management tasks within Kubernetes.

When working on these projects, document your process, configurations, and challenges faced. Create a GitHub repository or portfolio website to showcase your projects, including code, architecture diagrams, and explanations. This hands-on experience will not only demonstrate your Kubernetes skills but also serve as valuable examples to discuss during interviews.

www.ingramcontent.com/pod-product-compliance
Lightning Source LLC
LaVergne TN
LVHW051742050326
832903LV00029B/2676